I0825194

Praise for *The Rule of Three*

"This book will help identify and close gaps toward achieving the value potential of your business. Bill Canady is a seasoned CEO and has the battle scars to prove it."

– Alan Fortier, President, Fortier & Associates

"If Canady's first two books were about sharpening the sword, this one is about forging the wielder—and recognizing that the most lethal weapon is actually a three-person strike team moving with synchronized purpose. The book's genius lies in making the abstract concrete: He doesn't just tell you that you need a Prophet to 'evangelize the vision'; he shows you exactly what that looks like through Zero-Up analyses, Quad Charts, and PDCA feedback loops that transform conceptual strategy into operational reality. For anyone who's ever inherited a turnaround mandate, assembled a transformation team, or wondered why brilliant strategies keep dying in the execution phase, *The Rule of Three* isn't just recommended reading—it's required scripture. Bill Canady has given us the missing manual for building teams that don't just survive transformation—they thrive in it."

– Todd Hagopian, COO, Player One Energy

"*The Rule of Three* landed with me much the same way a strong candidate does in a good interview—clear, confident, and grounded in real experience rather than theory. What stood out immediately was how straightforward the framework is. No theatrics, no over-polished abstractions. Just a practical operating model for aligning vision, execution, and accountability in a way that actually holds up under pressure. *The Rule of Three* is a strong contribution to modern leadership thinking. It brings clarity where there's usually noise and gives leaders a practical language for driving results. If you're responsible for growing or stabilizing an organization, this is absolutely worth your time."

– Mitchell Aiello, President and CEO, Boyd Corporation

"This book captures what truly drives sustainable success: clear vision, disciplined execution, and aligned leadership. Bill Canady delivers a powerful blueprint for any CEO focused on growth, accountability, and results."

– Adam Gibbs, CEO, OHIO Transmission Corporation

"*The Rule of Three* builds on Bill's prior books to reinforce the need for focused data-driven decision-making in a world drowning in data. The practical tools and framework make it a valuable resource for anyone looking to optimize profitability and drive sustainable growth."

– Eric Buechele, 80/20 Leader, Strategy Deployment, Organizational Change

"I've been through Lean, Six Sigma, and EOS—none of them address human alignment issues like *The Rule of Three*. It's a revelation for how leadership actually functions. This is the best leadership book I've read in years."

– Joe Ayette, MBA, Vice President, Operations Executive

"Bill Canady delivers a master class in leadership with *The Rule of Three*. This book is a game changer for anyone serious about building unstoppable businesses. Canady's central insight, that every thriving organization depends on three aligned roles—the Visionary, the Prophet, and the Operator—is both elegant and actionable. By showing how these roles work together to turn strategy into results, he gives leaders a clear road map for driving profitable growth and avoiding the chaos of misalignment. If you want clarity, focus, and a proven system for scaling success, this book belongs on your desk."

– Monique Verduzco, Chief Strategy Officer, WPS

"As a young founder, I'm constantly searching for actionable guidance, not just theory. Bill is that guide. He gives a clear system for making your business as profitable as possible. The 'Zeroing-Up' concept alone was a game-changer. This is a must-read for all entrepreneurs."

– Nick Mullin, Founder and CEO, Strategic Influence

THE RULE OF THREE

Also by Bill Canady

The 80/20 CEO: Take Command of Your Business in 100 Days

From Panic to Profit: Uncover Value, Boost Revenue, and Grow Your Business with the 80/20 Principle

THE RULE OF THREE

How Visionaries, Prophets, and Operators Make Your Business Unstoppable

BILL CANADY

Matt Holt Books
An Imprint of BenBella Books, Inc.
Dallas, TX

Matt Holt is an imprint of BenBella Books, Inc.
8080 N. Central Expressway
Suite 1700
Dallas, TX 75206
benbellabooks.com
Send feedback to feedback@benbellabooks.com

BenBella and *Matt Holt* are federally registered trademarks.

Printed in the United States of America
10 9 8 7 6 5 4 3 2 1

Library of Congress Control Number: 2025046893
ISBN 978-1-63774-906-7 (hardcover)
ISBN 978-1-63774-907-4 (electronic)

Copyediting by James Fraleigh
Proofreading by Sarah Vostok and Martha Gallant
Text design and composition by Jordan Koluch
Cover design by Jason Arias
Printed by Lake Book Manufacturing

For my mom and dad, who made me who I am.
Your love, sacrifice, and example still guide me every day.
And for my sister, whose strength and support remind me where
I came from and what truly matters.

Contents

PART I

THE POWER OF THREE . . .

Chapter 1

CHANGE LEADERSHIP

"Avoid organizational rigor mortis."

—Joel E. Ross and Michael J. Kami,
Corporate Management in Crisis: Why the Mighty Fall (1973)

Of two facts, there could be no doubt.

First fact: The Boeing B-29 Superfortress was a magnificent aircraft, the most advanced heavy bomber of World War II. It was bigger and had greater range, carried more bombs, attacked from higher altitudes, flew faster, and defended itself and its aircrews more effectively than any other bomber in the Pacific Theater of World War II, Allied or Japanese. Technologically, it was the most innovative bomber built to date, featuring a fully pressurized cabin, the most advanced instrumentation, the latest iteration of the top-secret yet already legendary Norden bombsight, and four .50-caliber two-gun turrets, which were remote controlled using an analog computer-directed fire-control system operated by just one gunner and a fire-control officer. The specs—altitude (31,850 feet), bomb capacity (as much as 44,000 pounds), speed (357 mph), and operating range (3,250 miles)—had all been drawn up for one purpose: to win the war across the vast distances of the Pacific.

Figure 01-01

A factory-fresh B-29 bound for the 504th Bombardment Group on November 1, 1944.

Second fact: Major General Haywood Hansell, who in August 1944 became commander of the XXI Bomber

Command and its B-29 fleet on the island of Saipan in the western Pacific, was a superb officer and one of the principal architects of the doctrine and tactics of high-altitude precision bombing. Considered a giant of military aviation, he was a Visionary.

All successful high-ranking leaders—leaders with command responsibility, whether in the military, government, or business—are Visionaries. We will define this term in greater detail later, but let me briefly explain my use of it here. Set aside any connotation of "visionary" as a dreamer of gauzy dreams and fantastic utopias. In the context of war, government, or business, the Visionary is the person who creates the quite literal vision of reality as it applies in all contexts relevant to the combat force, political entity, or company the Visionary leads. It is the job of the Visionary, having created the vision, to communicate it to subordinate leaders as the *mission* of the entity for which they serve or work. These subordinate leaders in turn create the strategy and the means of its execution so that the vision will be realized and the mission accomplished. In a combat force, the Visionary is a top commander (a senior general or admiral); in government, the emperor or empress, king or queen, prime minister, or president; in business, typically the CEO. For our purposes, however, we won't focus on specific business titles. The top commander of the business is the Visionary.

The Visionary's most immediate subordinate is what we

will call the Prophet—or Prophets, because there may be more than one. Often (but not invariably) the chief operating officer (COO) is the organization's Prophet, whose role is to acquire and maintain the deep understanding and expertise required to interpret, represent, and disseminate the Visionary's vision to other executives in the organization. The Prophet has the main task of training, coaching, and mentoring other key leaders to deploy a whole-of-business strategy to guide the realization of the vision and the mission aligned with it.

These key leaders whom the Prophet enables are those we call the Operators. These folks are typically the heads of constituent companies or leaders of major business units. Taking their direction from the Visionary, they act upon the Prophet's instruction and counsel to create a strategy specific to their business unit to execute the vision as that unit's mission.

Now, let's get back to General Hansell, his XXI Bomber Command, and the unit's B-29 fleet on Saipan. For there was a third fact: The magnificent, supremely advanced B-29s were not hitting their targets in Japan. Everything about the B-29 was designed for the precision bombing of specifically chosen targets from the relative safety of very high altitudes. As the Visionary, Hansell shaped his vision into a mission to execute raids on the Japanese factories that were producing weapons of war. The logic was simple: Destroy the factories, and destroy Japan's ability to continue waging war.

Figure 01-02

Brig. Gen. Haywood S. Hansell was a fine US Army Air Forces commander, who nevertheless failed to understand his mission.

This vision—one Hansell shared with numerous other Allied military leaders—was of total victory without the necessity of total annihilation. Strategically and morally economical and efficient, it was a vision of warfare in harmony with the values of democratic nations, especially the United States, that were opposed to mass murder committed even under the color of national interest. Certainly, it was a value General Hansell cherished and embraced, along with another value highly prized by commanders serving enlightened democratic republics: to protect to the extent possible the lives of the troops under your command. With his men flying in bombers bristling with defensive weapons at an altitude beyond the reach of most Japanese fighter aircraft and ground-based antiaircraft artillery, Hansell was confident that they were protected. His vision, and thus his conception of his mission, was driven by two intimately related values: Avoid mass murder of enemy noncombatants while preserving the lives of those he commanded.

Hansell's first assignment was to wipe out Japan's aviation industry. It started on November 24, 1944, with a raid on the Nakajima Aircraft Company (which today makes Subaru cars). The B-29s performed as they were designed to, coming in over Tokyo at an altitude safe from enemy fighters and artillery. The result? Intensive bombing by 40 B-29s damaged just 1% of the Nakajima plant. Hansell quickly launched a second raid with twice as many B-29s, which again bombed from almost 32,000 feet. And mostly missed. At this altitude, they were bombing into what meteorologists would later dub the jet stream, a broad river of air that tears through the upper atmosphere like rapids in a river.

Because nothing could be done about the jet stream,

Army Air Forces commanders urged Hansell to abandon precision bombing and use a new munition, napalm—murderous jellied gasoline—to carpet-bomb Tokyo. Mostly built of combustible wood and paper, the city was the perfect target for an incendiary raid. Resorting to what he considered mass murder—indiscriminate terrorism against a civilian population—would violate one of the chief values that had guided Hansell's vision and conception of his mission.

Was Hansell wrong about carpet bombing with napalm? No. It is truly a weapon of mass destruction, especially when deployed in massive amounts to wipe out an entire city, combatants and noncombatants: men, women, kids, granddads, grannies—everyone. But Hansell's assigned mission was to end a war that had already killed millions, combatants and noncombatants alike, across a large portion of the world. Total US combat casualties in the war against Japan were 111,606 killed and 253,142 wounded, about half of these in the closing months. At that point, Japan's military position was hopeless, as all Japan well knew, but its army and navy continued nevertheless to fight. America and its allies now believed that only the threat of total annihilation would halt the loss of life, theirs as well as Japanese. No one would have claimed that carpet bombing Japan was a *good* thing to do, but virtually all Allied military officers and government officials believed it was now the *only* thing to do.

Even Hansell recognized that he was losing at least one B-29 (and its crew of eleven) on every essentially futile high-altitude bombing mission he launched. Morale wasted away, and his officers were turning against him. At last, General Lauris Norstad, deputy to General Henry "Hap" Arnold, the Army Air Forces chief, directly ordered Hansell to launch a major napalm attack on the city of Nagoya. Hansell responded half-heartedly with a small-scale "trial" raid, which burned three acres of the city. Norstad discounted this as a mere pinprick and, flying from Washington to Guam, met there with Hansell on January 6, 1945, and bluntly informed him that he was being replaced by Major General Curtis Emerson LeMay.

Why was Hansell fired? Because this Visionary's vision conflicted with the vision of Visionaries at higher levels, Arnold and his deputy Norstad. In war, if your mission does not perfectly align with high command's vision, you will likely suffer Hansell's fate. In government, if your mission drifts from what the electorate put you in office to accomplish, you will likely not gain reelection. In business, if your mission and vision are misaligned, you, the business, or both will suffer.

Hansell's vision created a mission driven by two humanitarian values: minimizing civilian casualties and aircrew losses. Arnold and Norstad's vision created a mission to win the war against Japan by any means necessary. During the Civil War, Confederate cavalry commander Nathan Bedford Forrest concisely defined his vision of war and the mission required to execute it. "War," he said, "means fighting, and fighting means killing." The words of this Confederate general could well have been uttered by Hansell's replacement.

Curtis LeMay had a richly deserved reputation as a taskmaster, relentlessly drilling his pilots and crews to make their missions more effective and boost the grim odds of their survival. The tactics he instilled in them were based on his close observations and the analysis of data gathered from rigorous damage assessments and meticulous crew debriefings after each mission.

Figure 01-03

Gen. Curtis LeMay, the Visionary who redefined the mission of the B-29 in winning the Pacific War, seen here in the late 1950s, shortly after the award of his fourth star.

In 1929, LeMay had joined what was then called the United States Army Air Corps while he was studying civil engineering at The Ohio State University—importantly, he was an engineer first and an aviator second. He understood the study of stresses on structures, on dynamic systems of cause and effect, and on what measurements and their analysis could reveal about the behavior of physical objects in a physical world.

Despite facing tremendous pressure to succeed immediately where Hansell had failed, LeMay approached his mission as an engineer would. He decided to attack the same Nakajima aircraft plant that had hastened the end of Hansell's command. Albert Einstein is credited with having said, "Insanity is doing the same thing over and over again and expecting different results." But LeMay knew he had to prove whether the failure against Nakajima was Hansell's or something else. So, in January and February 1945, he sent more than a hundred B-29s to bomb the plant. It survived very much intact.

Now LeMay had the data he needed. The problem wasn't Hansell. LeMay had adjusted the mission as much as he could by adding more aircraft. Something more radical had to be tried.

He understood that he faced two tyrants. One was the weather. This region was often cloudy. The fabled Norden bombsight was useless if the bombardier could not see through the cloud cover. Besides the clouds, the jet stream was blowing the bombs off target, especially when released from high altitude.

The other problem was the magnificent B-29s themselves. They had been built for unprecedentedly high-altitude daytime bombing. Billions of dollars had been devoted to attaining this literally lofty goal. But to free himself and his crews from the tyranny of the weather, LeMay had to confront the second tyranny of the B-29's design. He therefore decided that they had to bomb from a much lower altitude, between 5,000 and 9,000 feet—and below both the jet stream and the clouds. He realized that he could not let the plane's design—crafted to protect crews by enabling them to attack from 30,000 feet—force him to order futile missions. Still, sending crews in low during daylight would be suicidal. At 5,000 feet, the fully visible giant B-29s would be vulnerable both to defending fighter planes and the dense rings of ground-based antiaircraft guns encircling every Japanese city.

So, LeMay had to craft a new vision. The bombers would approach low, but at night, under cover of darkness. This immediately ruled out precision-bombing any particular target as Hansell had. Instead, LeMay attacked the cities of Japan themselves, beginning with Tokyo in March 1945. The munition of choice? Napalm—as much as each bomber in each mission could carry. LeMay had every pound of unnecessary weight removed from the bombers. He took out all the guns—the ones intended to make the Superfortress genuinely *super*, immune to fighter attack—leaving only the tail cannon. Stripping the armament also saved on the weight of the gunner and fire control officer, along with their heavy belts of .50-caliber ammo. LeMay further ordered that the bottom surfaces of each B-29 be painted flat black, to blend in with the night sky—he had no wish to send his men on a suicide mission. Nevertheless, when the flight crews were briefed on their new duties, many accepted that they were now dead men and wrote farewell letters to wives and families.

Hansell had operated from a vision driven by a value that prized crew safety and minimized noncombatant deaths above all else. LeMay, in contrast, operated from only one value: achieving total victory. The realities of the situation in which his vision and mission were to be achieved required him to discard the technological "advantages" of the B-29—high operational ceiling and multiple defensive guns—to thwart the weather's effect on the operation. Even more radically, he rejected Hansell's humanitarian value of avoiding mass murder through precision bombing. Freed from that vision, LeMay decided to carpet-bomb entire Japanese cities with napalm, a munition especially suited to cities built extensively from inflammable materials as Tokyo was. The firebombing of Tokyo on March 9–10, 1945, annihilated nearly 16 square miles of the city and rivaled the civilian casualties of the atomic bombs over Hiroshima and Nagasaki that coming August.

LeMay understood that the mission was not to protect

the warriors but to ensure that their efforts would be productive. This mission would be achieved by inflicting sufficient destruction on the enemy to end World War II, even if the definition of *enemy* included noncombatants. As LeMay himself explained following the war, we "had to have results, and I had to produce them. If I didn't produce them, or made a wrong guess, get another commander in there. That's what happened to Hansell. He got no results. You had to have them."

Data, analysis, action, results. This was all that mattered to Curtis LeMay in evaluating both Hansell's dismal results and then the results of his own radically different vision of the mission. The results would produce more data to be analyzed so that the next action could be modified to produce even better results. In LeMay's mind, you had to accept risk and cost—not surrender to avoidable tyrannies. You couldn't stop the jet stream and you couldn't disperse the clouds, but you could evade their tyranny by using your weapon in a way it was never meant to be used.

Earlier in the war, when LeMay was commanding bombing forces in Europe, he had ordered another radical departure from the tyranny of accepted practice. Bombing doctrine dictated that the planes take continuous evasive action as they approached their targets. This made it harder for ground-based antiaircraft fire to hit them, but it also reduced their bombing accuracy while greatly increasing flying time over enemy territory. LeMay knew that going straight in would improve accuracy, and he also reasoned that the reduced exposure to enemy fire would actually make crews safer, even though flying straight in made them sitting ducks.

Deciding to put his own skin in the game by sharing his flight crews' risk, LeMay led the first straight-in mission over Germany himself. He did not accompany the missions he directed against Japan. Had he lost his nerve? Probably not. In Europe, he was just one of several important commanders and understood that he was readily replaceable. In the Pacific Theater, attacking the capital of the enemy, he understood that he and he alone was *it*. LeMay knew that he could be relieved of command, but he did not feel that he could be replaced. No one else would have interpreted the data as he had. No one else would have sent the precious B-29s and their even more precious crews into combat in ways so contrary to all the accepted assumptions. No one else, therefore, could have performed the mission as he ordered it to be performed.

VISIONARY, PROPHET, OPERATOR

In leading the air war against Japan at the end of World War II, Curtis LeMay was a Visionary. But the men he led never called him that. Their nickname for him was considerably less romantic: "Iron Ass." Some historians think the label was actually an expression of pride and, in some ways, gratitude. He drove his command very hard. He ordered them to do things some thought suicidal. Had it all gone wrong,

LeMay's tactics would in fact have been suicide. But *data, analysis, action, results* gave Iron Ass a strikingly clear vision of the mission at hand and an emphatically counterintuitive, unconventional, but totally data-driven vision of how that mission *must* be accomplished.

LeMay had good reason not to risk personally leading the low-altitude Japanese missions, as he had earlier led the straight-in missions over Germany. He certainly never called himself "visionary" or "indispensable." But he was both: an indispensable visionary who accomplished the mission his predecessor had failed to accomplish. He also must have known that no other leader who might be sent to replace him would see the mission as he saw it, much less order its execution.

LeMay's decision not to fly with his men *this* time tells us something else. A visionary leader is indispensable, necessary to success. But a visionary leader is not sufficient. LeMay had confidence in his subordinate leaders, if for no other reason than that he had coached them relentlessly enough to deserve being called Iron Ass. Like any large military organization, the XXI Bomber Command had numerous cascading subordinate commands. The unit was composed of wings, which were composed of groups, which were, in turn, composed of squadrons. The wing and group commanders had the unenviable job of inculcating in the squadron commanders the operational aspects of LeMay's vision. If LeMay was the Visionary, his wing and group leaders were his evangelical Prophets.

Ultimately, it was the squadron commanders who implemented the vision the wing and group leaders conveyed to them. The squadron commanders might be called the Operators. They piloted the lead planes in their squadrons, and it was up to them to coordinate the attack on the mission's target in real time.

LeMay knew that no military commander can, by simple fiat, impose his vision on the officers and enlisted personnel of his command. The Visionary's vision had to be realized, made real, through leadership at two principal lower levels, Prophets and Operators. Without the informed and inspired alignment of all three leader categories—Visionary, Prophet, and Operator—the bold and dangerous mission LeMay had envisioned for defeating Japan would surely have failed, as it had failed under his predecessor.

BELOW TOP BILLING

Visionaries always get top billing, but they would never even make it onto the marquee without the Prophets and Operators. A Visionary whose vision is not enacted is like a composer whose music is never performed.

In Judeo-Christian theology, God is the Visionary but Moses is the Prophet—a role Jesus assumes in the New Testament. In Islam, "Allah is God, and

Mohammad is his Prophet." God the Visionary may create the universe but does not create the religion through which God is worshipped. Founding religions is the role of the Prophets. Running religions day to day in alignment with the word of the Prophets is the role of rabbis, priests, and imams—the Operators of religious belief.

This example uses religion as its model, but the same dynamic operates in most successful organizations. For the Visionary LeMay, commanding the XXI Bomber Command in the Pacific Theater, his Prophets were the commanders of groups within the XXI, and his Operators were the commanders of the squadrons within the groups. In America's War of Independence, George Washington was the Visionary architect of the Continental Army and its strategy. His vision was often flawed in its details, but it ultimately kept the army together and defeated the British forces. His Prophet was young Alexander Hamilton—often described as Washington's right-hand man—who faithfully disseminated Washington's vision and provided a feedback loop to the general. As president, Washington was without question the Visionary who created a durable model of the nation's chief executive, and he appointed Hamilton as his first secretary of the

Treasury. In this role, Hamilton was the Prophet who, aligned with Washington's vision, created a financial structure that would enable the execution of all that a government does. In Washington's cabinet, Hamilton also played the role of Operator, along with the other original cabinet-level appointees: Attorney General Edmund Randolph, Secretary of State Thomas Jefferson, and Secretary of War Henry Knox. These Operators led their departments on a day-to-day basis.

Remember that the titles *Visionary, Prophet,* and *Operator* apply to roles rather than people. Depending on context and situation, a Visionary may play the role of Prophet or even Operator. LeMay was the Visionary of the XXI Bomber Command, but in the context of the entire Army Air Force, he was the Prophet in service to General Hap Arnold. During the Cold War, LeMay might be considered the Visionary behind the Berlin Airlift. Recognizing that his expertise was in bomber strategy, he soon turned over the top leadership of that epoch-making operation to a logistics expert, Lieutenant General William H. Tunner, and became head of the Strategic Air Command, which, in true Visionary fashion, he recreated as the nation's principal nuclear strike force.

Data, analysis, action, and *results* drive the vision of the Visionary, who conveys the vision to the Prophets, who instruct and inspire the Operators, those leaders immediately responsible for executing the vision to produce the intended results.

THE UNDENIABLE POWER OF THREE

Curtis LeMay was a change leader. The change he led was from failure to success. The very first thing change leaders do is recognize the need for change. LeMay readily saw that his predecessor, General Hansell, "got no results." We "had to have results," LeMay reasoned, "and I had to produce them." From this reasoning, he set out to do what all successful change leaders do: create a vision for the future and inspire others to take action to make tomorrow different from today by producing the necessary results.

From studying the data, LeMay realized he had to use the B-29 radically differently from its designed purpose, discarding precision high-altitude daytime explosive bombing for nighttime incendiary carpet bombing from dangerously low altitudes. He presented this radical vision to his subordinate officers, the wing and group commanders—his Prophets. They, in turn, directed, mentored, and coached the Operators, the commander-pilots who led the attacking squadrons.

Given the B-29's intended purpose, Curtis LeMay's vision was innovative, bold, and risky—the product of extreme change leadership. But while this Visionary's vision was new, the processes through which he conceived and executed it were extremely well established.

First, he built his vision on *data, analysis, action,* and *results.* Adherence to these liberates a leader from such false tyrannies as surrendering to the weather and clinging to high-altitude bombing just because the B-29 was designed for it. Thus liberated, LeMay focused on the only goal that mattered: accomplishing the mission by getting the needed results. As for executing his vision, he fully exploited the holy trinity of leadership, playing the role of Visionary and then disseminating that vision to the organization through Prophets and Operators.

If you have the sense that good things come in threes, you are not alone. There is an old saying—and we know it is really old because it was expressed in Latin—that goes "*Omne trium perfectum,*" which translates as "Everything that comes in threes is perfect." The New Testament departed from the Old by introducing not a single God but a Holy Trinity. Wiccans, practitioners of a pagan, earth-centered faith, believe that the energy a person projects into the world returns to them threefold.

A diverse array of professions observe a diverse array of practices they all call a "Rule of 3." C++ software programmers observe a Rule of 3 concerning class method definitions. Pilots calculate their rate of descent using a Rule of 3 equation in which the factors are Descent, Altitude, and Travel Distance. Hematologists have a Rule of 3 that ensures the accuracy of blood counts. Biochemists apply a Rule of 3 to determine the presence of lead and lead-like compounds in tissue. Survivalists have a Rule of 3 to prioritize survival steps to take.

Perhaps the most familiar manifestations of the Rule of 3 is the profusion of plots and storylines that center on three. It's not "The Four Little Pigs," "Goldilocks and the Two Bears," *The Six Musketeers*, or "A Dozen Coins in the Fountain," right? Sloganeers love to formulate their sayings in threes. We've got "Life, liberty, and the pursuit of happiness," "Stop, look, and listen," "Stop, drop, and roll," "Turn on, tune in, drop out," "Snap, Crackle, and Pop," and "Government of the people, by the people, for the people." When you need encouragement more specific than "If at first you don't succeed, try, try again," you recite, "Third time's the charm."

Movies? Try *Three Days of the Condor*; *One, Two, Three*; *The Three Amigos*; *A Letter to Three Wives*; *The Three Faces of Eve*; and *Three Men and a Baby*.

The Founding Fathers had abundant faith in the Rule of 3. The US dollar bill depicts both sides of the Great Seal of the United States, the obverse dominated by an American bald eagle and the reverse dominated by a pyramid, the solid embodiment of a triangle. More significantly, the entire structure of the American democratic system of government is founded on the Rule of 3, with power divided among the legislative, executive, and judicial branches, which work together and yet oppose each other in what we call "the system of checks and balances."

With the evidence so abundant for the Rule of 3's compelling power, any business that needs or wants to profitably grow not only needs a top leader with a vision but, just as important, must be willing to commit to that vision across the entire organization. This means applying the Rule of 3 and ensuring that the organization has a Visionary along with one or more Prophets and a sufficient cadre of Operators, all of whom are necessary for fully aligning the entire organization to successfully execute on the CEO's vision.

THREE TO TANGO

Visionary, Prophet(s), Operators. It takes three roles—and the people to play them—to successfully run *any* company. I say "any" company because there are millions of companies offering a wide variety of things or services. Each firm is a unique beast that requires special care and feeding. This said, there are only three essential *types* of companies:

1. **The Values company.** The Values company is often a private company, and its values are those of the owner. Typically, a values-driven company is a historically successful enterprise that has allowed a higher calling, a sense of a new values-centered mission, to distract its leadership from whatever had made it successful in the first place.

To be sure, not all values-driven companies fail. Far from it. Subaru, for example, sponsors programs that devote a portion of sales revenue to financing environmental programs, a practice featured in its advertising. Subaru also happens to make fairly priced automobiles known for their safety and reliability. Concern for the environment is an extension of a brand that burnishes its image of social responsibility. The value contributes positively to the appeal of product and enhances profitability. An even more iconic brand, the Hershey Company, began as a private company in 1894 but has been a public corporation since 1927. Its founder and longtime owner, Milton S. Hershey, allocated a huge amount of value to funding orphanages, an industrial school in Hershey, Pennsylvania, and other charitable ventures. The M. S. Hershey Foundation, established in 1935, continues to advance Hershey philanthropy and is partly financed by shares in the corporation. It is, however, wholly independent, and thus its values do not drive corporate financial decisions. Hershey ranks fourth worldwide among confectionary companies. This is unquestionably a success, but it is also true that the number one worldwide confectioner, Mars Incorporated, which remains family owned, has never been a values-driven enterprise.

We could compare General Hansell to the Visionary/CEO of a Values company because his vision for his mission prized humanitarian values: crew safety and avoiding excess noncombatant deaths above all else. In contrast, General LeMay is analogous to the Visionary/CEO of a Mission company.

2. **The Mission company.** These companies are driven by a very specifically defined goal. The clearest example is a company owned by private equity (PE), the assigned mission of which is typically to get a MOIC (multiple on invested capital) of three. Because it has a clearly defined mission, expressed in the language of business (which is money), this type of company is the easiest to run, high as the pressure to perform may be. In the Pacific Theater, LeMay shaped his vision to create a mission, whose success or failure was clearly measurable by the metric of total annihilation of the enemy. His predecessor's mission, based on his humanitarian values, produced measurable failure. LeMay changed the vision, the mission, and the means of execution by radically reconfiguring the B-29, the tactics by which it was flown, the weapons it deployed, and the objectives it targeted, to clearly measurable improvement.
3. **The Values & Mission company** is a public company that starts the quarter as a values-driven

business (the values being those of the stakeholders) and morphs into a mission-driven company by each quarter end. That is, values dominate in months one and two but are elbowed out of the way in month three by the mission, which is a dollar target pegged to the close of the quarter. Miss this, and heads will likely roll. Values & Mission companies are the hardest to run because of the built-in quarterly change in priorities. Some public companies, like the Starbucks Corporation, are forced to combine the two. Founder Howard Schultz had a values-based vision of a company that could bring the individualistic intimacy of the standalone coffeehouse to national chain scale. This worked well for a remarkably long time—until it didn't. We will discuss this further in chapter 6, but when vision and mission are misaligned, companies falter and—you guessed it—heads roll.

The company's type is the company's *why*, its reason for being. The company's *who* is the three-role team charged with running the enterprise successfully. I know that it takes three leaders (or three leadership roles) to successfully run any business: Visionary, Prophet(s), and Operators. My experience, plus the endless reiteration of these three roles through business history, tells us this is true, and there is ample data to support it.

THE MAGIC OF THREE

Provocative business author Malcolm Gladwell may be best known for his concept of the "tipping point." His follow-up to *The Tipping Point* (2007), titled *Revenge of the Tipping Point* (2024), draws on research by Harvard Business School professor Rosabeth M. Kanter to explain why building effective teams is not just a matter of throwing together people from diverse backgrounds and with diverse experience, shaking the concoction well, and then hoping for the best. Kanter found that tossing a woman into an all-male team and expecting magical results was insufficient. She concluded that a critical mass of women—or any other diverse or divergent "newcomer"—was required for each such newcomer to become effective within the team. Gladwell checked up on this insight: "I just called up a lot of women who were pioneers on corporate boards and asked them what it was like when they were the only woman on the board. And what it was like when there were three of them on the board, and they all gave the same answer, which is, as weird as it sounds, 'When I became one of three, the way I was treated and the way I behaved just fundamentally changed.'"

At this tipping point, both the treatment each newcomer *received* and the behavior each *manifested* changed and did so "fundamentally." This is why Gladwell calls this tipping point "The Magic Third." Add to the team three divergent members—three women, three engineers, three persons of color—and all three of this cohort are perceived as important and effective and, in fact, become capable of contributing to the team in important and effective ways.

Diversity is inherently valuable. Some companies value it for social reasons, even reasons of legal compliance; others value it for its inherent and proven utility in expanding a company's understanding of diverse markets. What is ineffective, even counterproductive, is hiring one representative of a particular background or perspective just to check off a box next to "diversity" and call it a day. A Magic Third—three of a kind—is required for the team's group dynamics to reach a productive critical mass. Gladwell concludes that the research on this is compelling and consistent, noting that the Magic Third applies to diversity in all categories—background, education, professional experience, race, nationality, gender, and so on.

THE VISIONARY

I will detail the roles of the three critical leaders in future chapters, but let's review them quickly here, starting with the Visionary.

Because the Visionary is the first and final decision maker within a business, this role typically coincides with that of the CEO. The CEO's power is rarely absolute, especially if the business has a board of directors. Moreover, if the Visionary/CEO decides to be guided by this book, she must commit herself to adhering to the Rule of 3—that is, ensuring complete alignment with the Prophet(s) and the Operators, who, reciprocally, must be deeply committed to the Visionary's vision.

Since the Visionary role normally coincides with that of the CEO, you may ask why we don't just call the Visionary by her corporate title. The reason is that the word *Visionary* conveys the central idea of *vision.* The Visionary CEO has—or acquires—a deep understanding of both the past and present state of the enterprise and, using data, sets a goal and envisions a plan for a desired future state.

Creating a vision is only one requirement for the Visionary. The vision of the business must not be a still photograph or a portrait in oils. It is a movie—in fact, a 3D action movie. The picture changes, fast, in real time. For this reason, the Visionary cannot be an oracle hidden in a remote cave but must be out and about as well as agile and highly focused. The Visionary creates the clearest and best vision possible, but it is, of course, a vision with many moving parts. Nor should it ever be imagined, much less presented, as a "finished" *state of perfection*. It must have a well-defined goal, but the vision itself is of real-life *progress* toward that goal—not of perfection. Like everything else in both life and business, the vision is subject to revision as it engages, through time and circumstance, with reality.

THE PROPHET(S)

You need a Prophet, quite possibly more than one. You cannot have a Prophet without a Visionary, but without a Prophet it is almost impossible for a Visionary to successfully deploy the vision. Prophets are typically senior C-suite executives, often in the COO function. They have the practical knowledge and know-how required to deploy the vision. That is, the Prophet translates the vision into actions, typically through training, coaching, and mentoring other executives, especially Operators, throughout the organization in the deployment of the company strategy.

Companies that are embarking on a change-leadership project can bring one or even a set of Prophets from the outside, as consultants and coaches, especially in such crucial areas as the application of the 80/20 Pareto Principle, which is central to all successful growth strategies and is discussed in detail in Part II of this book, along with other useful tools. This said, you cannot rent a Prophet for very long. The Rule of 3 must become organic to the business, lest its leaders and managers drift away from the required alignment. Experience shows over and over again that, without a Prophet organically embedded in the business, key personnel will inexorably regress from aligning on the growth strategy, including the rigorous discipline of 80/20. True, the Prophet is not the author of the company's Holy Writ—that's the Visionary's role—but the Prophet *is* the keeper, the interpreter, and the evangelist of the vision.

THE OPERATORS

The Operators are the leaders who run the business day to day. Often, this role corresponds to the company or business-unit title of *president*. In the kind of conglomerated businesses I have run as CEO during my career, Operators have been the presidents of business units or operating companies. They don't set the strategy, but they are charged with implementing and executing it within their special domains.

Operators are a source of ideas and innovations, but not of the overall, organization-wide strategy—again, that is the Visionary's task. Nor are they the keepers and masters of the practices and processes by which the vision is implemented as a mission; this is the domain of the Prophet. What they do have is practical, intimate working knowledge of their business units or companies. They must be thoroughly evangelized on the strategic vision and the processes and practices necessary to ensure their business is perfectly aligned with the strategy and meets or exceeds all its strategic goals, but their focus is deployment and application. They are the point people who bring the strategy to life.

WILL IT WORK?

If the Visionary bases their vision on data, analysis, action, and results, and if these are faithfully executed through Prophets and Operators in full alignment, the Rule of 3 that contributed mightily to the Allies' victorious outcome in the Pacific Theater will no doubt help any business that seeks to achieve and sustain profitable growth.

The next three chapters of Part I provide greater operational detail for the Visionary, Prophet, and Operator roles. While Part I is simply titled "The Power of Three . . . ," Part II is ". . . And How They Use It." Its five chapters provide the tools and processes necessary to strategically and tactically execute the three leadership roles. "Epilogue: Always Be Exiting" concludes the book by proposing a management approach very specifically aimed at growing the value of the business. It offers the management option of structuring and running the company as if you intend to sell it (whether or not this is your intention). The familiar salesman's mantra, ABC—"Always Be Closing"—becomes ABE: Always Be Exiting.

Chapter 2

VISIONARY

> "Give me a lever long enough and fulcrum on which to place it, and I shall move the world."
>
> —Archimedes

Every company needs a Visionary. *Visionary*, like *Prophet* and *Operator*, is a necessary business role. But you won't find "Visionary" on any corporate org chart. The closest you can come to it is CEO, which in most companies is the official corporate title of what I call the Visionary. In view of this, calling someone a "visionary CEO" may be intended as a great compliment, but it is actually redundant. Or should be regarded as such.

I once found myself seated at the bar of the Seelbach Hotel in Louisville, Kentucky, and made an embarrassing mistake.

"Pour me any really great Kentucky bourbon, neat," I asked the barkeep.

He narrowed his eyes and leveled them at me.

"All bourbon is Kentucky bourbon," he said in a low monotone I will never forget.

Figure 02-01

The legendary Rathskeller in the Seelbach Hotel, Louisville, KY.

Maybe that's why I am always tempted to respond to anybody who says something like, "Bill Gates was a visionary CEO" not with enthusiastic agreement but with a snarky question: "Aren't all CEOs visionary?" Not wanting to get a reputation for being a jerk (or something that rhymes with "tick"), I have never actually responded this way. But if I had, I bet the other person would shoot back with, "No, not every CEO." Then I could retort: "But they should be."

Fact is, all CEOs are either visionaries or should be, because if they are not visionary, they are not a real CEO, no matter what letters follow their name. Bill Gates, a CEO, was a Visionary. How do I know this? Because he personally wrote the vision that launched Microsoft into and through its first decade:

> "A Computer on Every Desk, in Every Home."

This was in April 1975, six years before IBM launched its Model 5150, the first "Personal Computer" (PC). When Gates wrote down his vision, IBM was certainly making computers, but they were all mainframes, like the iconic System/360, a room-sized collection of floor-standing components that included a central processing unit with a control panel, disk storage unit, tape drive, disk storage drive, printer with paper, and (usually) a card punch and card reader. Pretty much nobody had a System/360 in a room inside their house. Not only wouldn't it have fit, you'd have paid $253,000 for the typical configuration (Model 25), which could be leased for $5,600 a month. The highest-priced iteration, Model 195, was priced between $7 and $12.5 million. These are 1969 dollars; multiply by 8.71 to get a rough estimate of what that means in current dollars.

Figure 02-02

Missouri state officials huddle over the control console of an IBM 360 during the 1960s.

Now *that's* the point.

If you mentioned the word *computer* in 1975, the

vision this would summon in an executive's mind would be the numerous components of an IBM/360 arrayed in a very clean room with excellent air-conditioning. That was the present reality. But the visionary Gates did what visionaries have always done. He envisioned the future—or, more precisely, *a* future: one in which a computer sat on a desk.

That was just the first feature of his vision. It got much, much more consequential from there. In his full vision for his company, a computer was on *every* desk. Had he stopped there, it would have been a bold vision. But he did not stop there. He added "in every home." In 1975, to think of a desk was to envision an office in some big building downtown. Desks, like computers, needed a lot of office space. Gates not only envisioned the computer on a desk, but a desk located in a home. If your home lacked a desk, it could be on a kitchen table or any flat surface reasonably close to an electrical outlet. Gates's vision was of a future in which computers were ubiquitous and domesticated, like TVs and ovens and bathtubs.

To me, the most interesting aspect of the Visionary Gates's vision was that he created it *for a company that was not in the computer-making business*! It was in the software business. Most importantly, the software it focused on most intently was MS-DOS, the Microsoft Disk Operating System, which was developed to run the computers that would be made by IBM and, soon, other firms as well. He saw his company enabling a future of omnipresent personal computers (something that did not yet exist) by supplying the software to run them, the software to make these machines useful and, in fact, necessary.

With a single sentence fragment, Bill Gates envisioned a business in the future, with remarkable detail in so few words. (For the record, before Microsoft developed MS-DOS for the PC, it developed a version of the BASIC programming language for the Altair 8800 microcomputer manufactured by Micro Instrumentation and Telemetry Systems [MITS]. The first computer Microsoft manufactured under its own name was the Microsoft Surface, a series that did not debut until October 2012.)

A DEEPER VISION

If you want to explain to somebody what a Visionary does, just reel off "A Computer on Every Desk, in Every Home." But if you're inclined to dig deeper than a sentence fragment for your vision, turn to Gates's competitor and nemesis, Steve Jobs.

Jobs came up with an imperative sentence that was even shorter than Gates's fragment. "Think different" was an ad slogan and logo Apple ran from 1997 to 2002. Its genius was in its apparent departure from "correct" grammar, transforming the adverb *differently* into . . . what? An adjective?

Not really. It was more like a noun in that it identified a *thing*, a quality of difference. The two-word sentence was an imperative to think—to envision—not the same thing others envisioned but different things. Apple was all about "different," as in different from IBM and its Microsoft-enabled PC.

Figure 02-03

Rival founders of the digital era Steve Jobs (left) and Bill Gates at the D5: All Things Digital Conference in Carlsbad, CA, 2007. What's behind those smiles?

Now, "Think different" was not so much Jobs's vision as it was a command intended to prompt both his company and its customers to *embrace* his vision. DOS for the IBM PC was the product of Bill Gates's vision, and it made personal computing possible. It established the whole product and technology category of the personal computer.

When Jobs applied the imperative *Think different* to this category, he revealed, drove, and realized a vision markedly different from Gates's: to create a company that focused less on customer needs and wants than on their pain points.

The IBM/Microsoft PC created a whole new universe of computing, making PCs available to masses of people who would otherwise have no direct contact with computers—not when they were the size, cost, and complexity of the IBM/360. But even with the PC, there was a rub, a pain point. Its eager purchasers were obliged to learn the machine's text-based OS language, MS-DOS, to communicate with them. This was a major pain because the typed commands that made the PC do what you wanted it to do looked like the arcane, nerds-only programming and operating languages of "Big Iron," the room-sized mainframes that took a crew of experts to run. Because *users* had to learn the *PC's* language, they, too, were put in the position of serving the machine.

Jobs's vision was to create a company that, feeling its customers' pain, brought them instant relief. The Macintosh operating system was not text based but instead depicted visually as a "desktop" where simple icons represented the programs and files. Thanks to the use of a mouse—not available for early PCs—gone were the obtuse, hard to memorize control-key combination commands that the DOS operating system required. Gone were all those nonsensical vowel-starved letter combinations. Just move the pointer with the mouse and click a functional icon or two!

No more pain. Thank you, Apple! The machine is serving the human. You're my best friend forever. In fact, maybe that sums up Jobs's unstated underlying vision: *Apple is a company that makes more than customers. It makes BFFs.*

Incredibly, Jobs's vision drove more than just a single solution. It propelled into the world a parade of diverse products. Just as there was a time when using a computer meant memorizing strings of letters, so there was a long era in which you had to buy an entire album of songs to get the only one you really wanted to hear—and you had to go to the record store to do it. What a pain! Then Jobs drove the creation of the Apple iPod, which was fed by the Macintosh music player, iTunes.

The iPod was released in 2001. The iPhone debuted in 2007. Clearly, it was a different product from the iPod and a very different product from the Mac. *Clearly* different? Not so much. Not when you revert to the CEO's vision. The iPhone, like Apple's earlier innovations, was a response to customers' pain points. It was the touchscreen-based mobile smartphone that cut the landline cord forever. It was also, to a surprising degree, a handheld computer (a mini Mac), and it included most of the functionality of the iPod. Then it added a whole new feature: a pretty good camera that, over succeeding generations of iPhones, evolved into a truly great still and video camera, capable of extraordinary resolution. Ever regret not having your Nikon or GoPro when your baby suddenly took their first steps? Reach for your iPhone and record away. By the way, doubtless inspired (or goaded) by Apple, Bill Gates eventually created a "Usability Lab" at Microsoft to better understand and salve his customers' pain. Microsoft evolved from the text-based MS-DOS to Windows, an operating system built on a graphical user interface. No law says a Visionary must have one and only one vision. Successful CEOs adapt and change—an evolutionary act that often begins with their vision.

WHAT IS THE FUTURE?

The future is nonexistent because it has not yet happened. The most productive view of the future is as a space of possibility, for everything from greatness to catastrophe. You need to know, however, that whereas some people view the future with excitement, hope, confidence, and anticipation, others look toward it in fear and trembling.

What, then, is the future? For any business enterprise, the future is the domain of the Visionary.

Gates and Jobs were Visionaries who vividly conveyed their vision to their companies and customers. But while you must be a Visionary to be truly a CEO, you don't have to be a CEO to be visionary.

Figure 02-04

A modern depiction of Archimedes moving the earth with only a lever, fulcrum, and a place to stand.

Archimedes (c. 287–212 BC) was a Syracusan physicist, mathematician, astronomer, inventor, and engineer. He was also a Visionary, said to have proclaimed, "Give me a lever long enough and fulcrum on which to place it, and I shall move the world." Now *that* is a vision worthy of a Visionary. Here's why:

1. It is literally visual. It does not merely paint a picture, it makes a movie.
2. It is not a vague, gauzy image—something glimpsed through a glass darkly. Rather, it is both clear and comprehensive. We see a lever long enough and a fulcrum, as well as the powerful action enabled by these two components.
3. It proposes a worthwhile, exciting, inspiring, challenging, and remarkable goal: *to move the world.*

4. It envisions an innovation in which people can clearly see what sort of input produces the desired output.
5. It provides enough information to motivate and inform the creation of a strategy and its execution. While nobody, not in Archimedes' day or our own, would ever take the vision literally—that, armed with a long-enough lever and a fulcrum, you could move the world—the vision is sufficient to make people believe that, given these things, they could move anything very big and heavy. That is, you could multiply human strength manifold and, with the proper strategy, build great buildings and monuments, or perhaps just clear a huge boulder from the road.

Archimedes provides us with a template any Visionary can use. At bottom, it is about transforming the present state into a desired future state. Let's revisit that boulder blocking the road. You know you cannot lift it with your two fragile hands and puny arms. You could just accept the situation as immutable reality and turn back, or you could follow Archimedes' vision, obtain a lever "long enough" and a fulcrum, and move the boulder. This is the essence of the Visionary's role:

1. Present an understanding of the present state.
2. Present a vision of a desired future state.
3. Present a vision of the required journey from present to future.

Note that Archimedes does not specify the materials from which either the lever or the fulcrum should be fashioned. Most important, while he stipulates that the lever must be "long enough," he does not specify how long. These are issues for other members of Archimedes' "team" to figure out. Under leadership by the Rule of 3, the Visionary owns the vision—the goal and the changes it will bring—while the Prophet aligns the organization on that vision and provides expertise in the processes through which the vision will be realized as an executable strategy, and the Operators directly apply that strategy to their segments of the enterprise.

So, we return to the definition of the future. For the enterprise, it is the vision of the Visionary as realized through the aligned efforts of the Prophet and the Operators.

HOW VISIONARY DOES A VISIONARY HAVE TO BE?

A Visionary—again, usually the CEO—must have excellent rear-view vision (a thorough understanding of the company's history), present-day vision (a thorough understanding of current operations, operating environments, and the markets), and, yes, future vision. The last requires neither a crystal ball nor a Magic 8 Ball but does call for an ability to rationally extrapolate from the present state of the company, its markets, and other aspects of its environment the range of risks and rewards in a probable future state. There is nothing supernatural here, but the Visionary does need to be wide awake to the implications of present-day decisions—whether already made, being made, or being contemplated—for the company's future.

Here is an example of the extrapolation Visionaries must exhibit. An executive from the PE firm I work with asked me to evaluate the prospective acquisition of, let's say, an industrial widget maker. I looked it over and replied that it seemed like a minor tertiary company with a complex global footprint and rather low gross margins. Given the complex geopolitical environment into which we were then entering—a radical change of US presidential administrations—I said I didn't think it would be an easy value-creation opportunity, adding that if the firm decided to bid, it should bid low.

My executive pushed back, saying that he and his team saw an opportunity, despite the validity of my assessment. So, I listed the issues in greater detail:

1. Gross margin issue: Because we are dealing with cost of goods sold, the gross margin is always the hardest number to raise. The target company is already located in low-cost

countries, so it should have taken advantage of labor and material arbitrage to profit from price differences.

2. Complexity: Their footprint is huge for such a small company! It's hardest to close or relocate international locations because of stringent and restrictive local laws and tax implications.
3. Lack of pricing power: The target company appears to be a second-tier tertiary player. Historically, we have had the most success with acquiring premier/premium-priced product and service companies.
4. Tariffs and other political issues: We just elected a US president who is a champion of tariffs. He has made no secret of his intentions to put tariffs on everything. I would expect double-digit cost increases within 18 months on materials sourced from low-cost countries.

This is what I told the executive he had to believe to make this deal work:

1. We can successfully rationalize the footprint and labor issue—hard to do on an international basis because of laws and taxes.

2. The target company has poor sourcing capabilities. It is already in low-cost countries.
3. The target being a small, tertiary company, it might encounter pricing increases on raw material commodities. This means we should expect lots of aggressive competitors, eager to race us to the bottom.

None of my prose here is sweeping or "visionary" in the common understanding of the word, but it is all about looking at present conditions and deciding what their impact will likely be on the future, most essentially our future prospects of profit from this particular acquisition. This is the usual task of a CEO vision statement.

THE VISIONARY'S REMIT

I've always liked the word *remit* in the way the Brits use it: as a one-word definition of the area of activity assigned or entrusted to an individual. This seems to me more accurate than simply speaking of an individual's "responsibility." A *remit* is assigned or, more importantly, entrusted to an individual, which makes that person its owner and thus 100% accountable for its success or failure. For the Visionary, usually the CEO, this is an awesome burden to shoulder. It is true that the CEO is often subject to a board of directors, but the buck, for better or worse, both originates with and stops with this one executive. The presence of a board aside, among the triumvirate of the Rule of 3, the Visionary's authority is absolute, yet the Visionary is neither a dictator nor an autocrat. Each decision carries ethical, social, and financial consequences, for which the Visionary is rightly held accountable.

The Visionary's decisions should be unambiguous, yet the environment of business is dynamic, never static. An enterprise aspiring to growth also must be dedicated to continuous improvement, which means that all decisions are subject to further decisions that may revise some or all the preceding ones.

The word *visionary* is freighted with mystic connotations. It is best to ditch any soothsayer and wizard analogies that come to mind and embrace instead the root of *visionary*, which is *vision*. And when it comes to vision, the clearer the better. Your business does not need a mystic, a fortune teller, or a hunch player. Your visionary should excel at seeing—sharply. Great chess masters, like great military commanders, have a talent for rapidly understanding the situation on the board or battlefield before them. Napoleon, General Grant, and General Patton were very different commanders, but they shared one great talent, which the French call *coup d'oeil*. The phrase means something like "a glance that takes in a comprehensive view." Chess masters can look at the board and play out, in their mind, an entire game without touching a single piece. The great generals could look at a battlefield and envision all the possibilities in a single glance. Both plan out the battle accordingly.

The Visionary in a business that is guided by 80/20 analysis and the other processes of the 80/20 Profitable Growth Operating System (PGOS) must tune her vision within the dynamic context and environment in which a profitable growth strategy is deployed. Moreover, she must develop her vision within the guardrails of the 80/20 principle and use 80/20 analysis to assess progress toward the goal the Visionary has set.

OH, CAPTAIN! MY CAPTAIN!

In 1833, the Scottish historian Thomas Carlyle coined the term "Captains of Industry" to describe the powerful industrialists of the Industrial Revolution in the British Isles. "Captain" is an inadequate term for today's CEOs, who are not expected merely to navigate the often treacherous and certainly fickle waters of commerce and industry, but rather to embrace the role of Visionary and communicate the vision to others.

The work of the Visionary calls for clarity concerning what the enterprise stands for and aspires to. Unless the current CEO/Visionary is a founder, the enterprise's vision of identity and aspiration is built on understanding the history and culture of the company and its historical performance, especially over the preceding three years. Innovation, reinvention, and adaptation in the present are often called for, but an arbitrary break with the past is not. Almost always, an element of stewardship is involved in formulating and articulating the enterprise's vision. Still, innovation and adaptability are highly prized, and in today's often accelerated markets, these qualities are indispensable to a Visionary.

The Visionary is not to be confused with the spiritual and intellectual hermit. Reflection, not hermetic isolation, is required. The Visionary asks, *Why does the organization exist?* and then lists the problems it solves and the benefits it brings. The Visionary also envisions and communicates what positive impact the organization must make on the community and the world. The Visionary should affirm that their understanding of the enterprise absolutely aligns with its core strengths and purposes. Such reflection should be followed by a vivid vision of the future. In this, most Visionaries begin with a solitary, meditative thought process before engaging key organization stakeholders in further crafting the vision. Ultimately, the Visionary should consult executives, customers, and employees at all levels.

Once the vision has been formulated, it must be communicated. Communicating the vision to the Prophet and other key executives comes first. The Prophet(s) must be inspired and aligned. The most effective Visionaries achieve this alignment by telling great stories, which evoke a tomorrow that is both different and much better than today.

Even as the Prophet(s) enable realization of the vision

among the leadership throughout the company, the Visionary should continue to engage with them and other stakeholders to reinforce the vision during the long journey toward its realization. In doing this, the Visionary, as well as the Prophet(s) and the Operators, must open themselves to questions and feedback from stakeholders, including customers. The Visionary should not disappear after launching the vision but should lead by example, demonstrating behavior that aligns with the values and goals presented in the vision.

At least half the Visionary's work is communicating in an inspiring and motivating fashion. Yet the Visionary is not responsible for implementing the vision. Rather, they must inspire the Prophet or Prophets of the enterprise to lead the creation of an executable whole-of-company strategy and then align all executives and key personnel in its deployment. This is the subject of the next chapter.

Chapter 3

PROPHET

"The prophet himself stands under the judgment which he preaches. If he does not know that, he is a false prophet."

—Reinhold Niebuhr, *Beyond Tragedy* (1937)

A PE firm hired me to run as CEO a conglomerate of decentralized businesses they had acquired. It was a B2B enterprise with separate companies catering variously to medical, technology, and industrial business customers. There is nothing inherently evil about a conglomerate, provided that its constituents are each run on strategies that align seamlessly with the overall strategic vision of the business. The enterprise I was hired to lead, however, was thoroughly decentralized, with the presidents of each constituent company essentially going their own separate ways. Interestingly, they all professed a belief in the 80/20 approach, but its application stopped at the borders of their particular fiefdoms. An economist would call the result *suboptimization*, meaning that the business units focused on their own priorities with little or no regard to the larger organization. To put this in aerodynamic terms, the result was increased drag rather than increased lift... and I assure you that the airplane was struggling to remain aloft, much less ascend.

When I came on board as CEO, I assumed the role of Visionary and, in concert with my executive leadership team, articulated a turnaround vision for the entire enterprise. Acutely aware that we needed help to disseminate 80/20 uniformly across all the subsidiary companies, so that all the presidents would be speaking the same language and could thus align on the vision, I brought in outside consultant trainers to fully inculcate 80/20 rigor.

I was hopeful. But the results, across more than a year, fell far short of my hopes. Let me stress that our executives, including the individual company presidents, were competent and conscientious, and the same was true of the outside trainers. Nevertheless, the uneven and disappointing results the consultants produced quickly persuaded me that we had to internalize our 80/20 processes more fully. Creating the vital alignment with the vision of the Visionary—in this case, *me*—required a Prophet: an organic one, not a rent-a-Prophet. Our Prophet needed to be one of us.

The Prophet, whose corporate role is typically (though not necessarily) COO, is tasked with acquiring and maintaining the deep understanding and expertise required to interpret, represent, and disseminate the Visionary's vision to other executives in the organization. To repeat my earlier description, the Prophet is charged with training, coaching, and mentoring other key leaders throughout the organization to deploy the whole-of-business strategy intended to execute the vision laid out by the Visionary. In 80/20-driven enterprises, Prophets are black belts in 80/20 analysis and design, with the emphasis on segmentation and simplification. Because they are 80/20 masters, they own the business-wide training of PGOS, ensuring that everyone on the executive team understands how 80/20 works and is competent at interpreting 80/20 analysis and applying the results. High in the portfolio of the Prophet's roles is *training the trainers* with the objective of ensuring an organic, sustainable internal cadre of PGOS experts. These leaders circulate through the entire organization, training all team members in the key processes.

It is the Prophet's responsibility to disseminate—either directly or through the cadre she trains—80/20 tools and training to everyone who is in positions that impact costs and grow revenue. Why can't an outside consultant do this better? Experience, including my own, has shown that unless you have a Prophet who is integral with and organic to the organization, it is all but inevitable that executives, managers, and other key personnel will regress from alignment on the vision and revert to practicing what they individually believe is right. If the organization's Prophet or Prophets are organic to the business, expect to see significant progress toward the goal set in the business plan within three to five months. If the organization relies on outside consultants and trainers, it is unlikely that significant performance improvement will be seen in anything short of 18 months, and it may not stick once the consultants have left the building.

WHY BEING A ONE-MAN BAND IS A POOR CAREER CHOICE

Wikipedia tells me that the earliest known one-man bands were 13th-century people who played a "pipe" (a one-handed flute) and "tabor" (an early version of the snare drum) simultaneously. Despite a longevity of at least 800 years, however, the vocation of one-man band has a very limited horizon. First, one-man bands may be fun (if you are easily amused), but they don't sound very good. Second, they will never sound very good because their creative and sonic possibilities are few. Third, a one-man band is inherently unscalable because as soon as you go beyond one man, you are no longer a one-man band. Fourth, if an autograph seeker appears, the one-man band has no hands left with which to sign.

So, if you are serious about making music, you are going to take up one instrument at a time, and if you want to accompany yourself, that instrument will be a guitar or a piano you play with both hands, leaving your diaphragm, throat, and mouth free to focus on the song. Even Bob Dylan doesn't try to sing and play the harmonica at exactly the same time.

You can be successful in business as a solo act, but, barring a stroke of genius or a once-in-a-generation run of extraordinarily good luck, your ability to scale is severely limited. The Taylor

Swifts of this world are hyper talented and hyper few. Plus, they will be the first to tell you how a big chunk of their income is shared with a small army of professionals who make their success possible, including booking agents, business managers, wardrobe designers, backup singers and instrumentalists, arrangers, security people, private pilots, and bus drivers—just to name a few.

But isn't it possible, even in a big company, for everyone to be a leader? Couldn't one person combine the roles of Visionary, Prophet, and Operator?

I've just asked myself two different questions. The answer to the first depends on what you mean by "leader." The answer to the second is *no*—at least, not if you want your enterprise to succeed.

Visionaries, Prophets, and Operators each have leadership responsibilities, which are defined within the separate roles I discuss in this book. All three roles are essential. How do we determine who plays what role? As mentioned, the Visionary is usually the corporate CEO, the Prophet is often the COO or a member (or members) of the CEO's staff, and the Operators are typically the presidents of constituent companies or segments of the business. The reason for these typical assignments is that the CEO's chief function is (or should be) visionary—that is, strategic at the highest level; the COO's chief function is to operationally enable and align the business to realize the Visionary's vision; and the Operators have the intimate knowledge of their companies or units to create for them and execute within them strategies that advance the whole business toward its visionary goals.

Figure 03-01

Ramblin' Conrad, a one-man band street musician, has toured the world for more than 20 years.

ADMINISTERING A DOSE OF PREDICTABILITY

There is no guarantee that those who hold the positions of CEO, COO, and president are ideally suited to their Rule of 3 leadership roles. It therefore may be worthwhile for leaders to swallow a dose of predictability by taking an assessment to understand their own leadership traits and tendencies. This knowledge may aid them in working with one another and with their executives and managers.

In the 1920s, the American psychologist William Moulton Marston developed a model of behavior that identified four distinct dimensions. During the early 1970s, Inscape Publishing further developed this model into a "personal profile system" called DiSC: *Dominance, influence, Supportiveness*, and *Conscientiousness.* The theory of DiSC is that our behavior is influenced by a mixture of these four dimensions, with different ones expressed to different degrees across individuals under various circumstances. A person's overall behavioral style will be shaped most by whatever dimension or dimensions are most strongly present in them.

Figure 03-02

A man of many works, William Moulton Marston invented an early version of the polygraph ("lie detector"), cocreated Wonder Woman, and developed the prototype of the DiSC personality profile system.

People who score high in the Dominance (D) style will tend to be strong willed and strong minded. They don't like to let anything get in the way of achieving their goals. They are decisive. They are often impatient with others, feeling that they take too long to get going. They are reluctant to give in to objections. They like to make their own rules rather than be told what to do. They are direct, blunt, and speak their minds, even if what they say is negative and possibly hurtful. They are competitive and want to win, sometimes at all costs.

Those who strongly exhibit the Influence (I) style find it gratifying to associate and work with others. They are "people persons" who enjoy being on a team. Their focus tends to be positive and optimistic. Their demeanor is cheerful, and they are expressive, outgoing, and even demonstrative.

Those with strong Supportiveness (S) look for ways to be helpful. They believe it is important to be fair and reasonable, and while they may find it somewhat difficult to adapt to change, they will support it once persuaded that it is necessary. They are not risk takers but prefer to hold on to what they have rather than take chances. Supportive folks work well in a group, but they like to be in the background, working behind the scenes. They are conflict averse and want to fit in. In fact, they let others have their way rather than protest or argue. Put somewhat pejoratively, they often take a go-along-to-get-along approach.

Last, people who score high in the Conscientiousness (C) dimension are focused on doing things right. They think carefully and clearly about assigned tasks. They plan ahead, are detail oriented, and make few errors. They set high standards for themselves, strive to exceed them, and are unhappy if they fall short. (The danger here is that they may let the *best* become the enemy of the *good,* prizing perfection over progress.) They enjoy working alone or with those few they highly trust.

None of these behaviors are absolute. They are traits and tendencies, and their expression is highly dependent on situation and context. That said, they are clues to understanding, appreciating, and even predicting strengths and weaknesses in leadership and matching prospective leaders to prospective roles. Consider the behavioral traits that follow.

The Dominance behavioral trait is associated with:

Getting immediate results
Taking action
Accepting challenges
Making decisions quickly
Questioning the status quo
Solving problems

The Influence behavioral trait is associated with:

Contacting people
Verbalizing

Creating enthusiasm
Entertaining others
Optimism
Group participation

The Supportiveness behavioral trait is associated with:

Consistent, predictable performance
Patience
Desire to help others
Loyalty
Listening
Fostering a harmonious and stable work environment

The Conscientiousness behavioral trait is associated with:

Adhering to instructions and standards
Focusing on details
Evaluating pluses and minuses
Double-checking accuracy
Performing critical analysis
Applying a systematic approach

A good leader combines aspects of all these traits, but there are vanishingly few such Swiss Army knives in executive and managerial cadres. The best you can do is seek out the right mix of people, try to suit strengths to roles, and understand the behavioral tendencies of even the top leaders. Stop looking for a one-man band. Instead, create a symphony orchestra. But do note that CEOs—Visionaries—tend to embrace what those familiar with DiSC would be quick to recognize as a Dominance role. Prophets most need a blend of the Influence and Supportive behavioral traits. These traits are best leveraged when the Prophet is internal and fully organic to the organization. As for Operators, they, too, often score high in Dominance but may also have a strong streak of Conscientiousness.

The term *Prophet* has spiritual and religious connotations, of course. This is no accident. That said, in the context of business, *Prophet* should not be confused with *evangelist* or *chief evangelist*, a now-common term for marketing folks who take the lead in promoting products or services. This is not the job of our Prophet, whose function, nevertheless, is quite similar to the first-ever evangelist, Saint John, also called Saint John the Evangelist. One of the four writers of the Gospels, he is the reason that people who seek to convert others to Christianity, mainly by preaching, are still called *evangelists.*

Evangelists are the propagators of the faith—and that, in a nutshell, is what our Prophet does. The Visionary furnishes the Holy Writ. The Prophet interprets, facilitates, and evangelizes it. The Prophet possesses the Profitable Growth Operating System (PGOS) knowledge, understanding, insight, and tools, sharing these with executives and managers throughout the organization. Moreover, the Prophet is also charged with transforming others within the company into evangelists.

Not to carry the evangelist comparison too far, but the PGOS does at least faintly resemble a religion, one based on the Gospel according to Pareto. Like other religions, this gospel rests on the belief that there is only *One Right Way*: to embrace a strategic vision that focuses on, strategically allocates resources to, and, at last, executes the 20% of actions that create 80% of the company's revenue.

In sharp contrast to practically all religions, however, PGOS preaches a *One Right Way* that is subject to continual revision for the purpose of achieving incremental improvement, progress toward perfection. So, as Gospels go, the PGOS preached by our Prophet is super agile. The Rock of Ages was hard, but PGOS is resilient, fashioned around a set of core products, markets, and values with which the vision and business strategy are totally aligned. The Prophet evangelizes with the object of disseminating deep understanding of the core strategy and total commitment to it. All the organization's believers are to be aligned with and from the core. Nevertheless, the Prophet both honors and facilitates change and adaptation within the core strategy. The Gospel the Prophet preaches is never immune to surrounding reality, and it is precisely that reality for which the Operator or Operators in the business are accountable. This is the subject of chapter 4.

Chapter 4

OPERATOR

"The ultimate test of management is performance."

—Peter Drucker, *Management: Tasks, Responsibilities, Practices* (1974)

The PGOS works optimally only if all three roles in the leadership triumvirate are filled effectively. The Visionary delivers the vision for the entire organization; the Prophet (or Prophets) provide the training and mentoring needed to implement the vision, aligning the entire organization on it; and the Operators, the business and division leaders throughout the enterprise, create and execute within their units a strategy that aligns with the vision for the entire organization. All three roles are indispensable. Without a Visionary, there obviously is no vision. Without a Prophet or Prophets, there are no leaders to guide the execution of the vision throughout the organization, using PGOS and applying 80/20. The Operators take their direction from the Visionary and, with the Prophet's instruction, guidance, and mentoring, implement it through a strategy specific to their business units. Without the Operators, the work of both the Visionary and Prophet could not be enacted and would therefore come to nothing.

THE DANGER OF SUBOPTIMIZATION

An Operator typically holds the corporate title of president and runs a constituent company or other business unit at a day-to-day level. Operators own the strategy of their companies or business units but are charged with ensuring that their strategy aligns with that of the whole company and continuously progressing toward the goal of the overall business plan. An Operator who fails to align strategy with execution at the business-unit level creates suboptimization. An all-too-common outcome in multi-unit businesses, suboptimization imposes a drain and drag on the enterprise because the leaders in the constituent business units have optimized for their own goals without regard for the overall impact on progress toward the common, whole-of-enterprise goal.

In some organizations, the Operators are not presidents but members of the CEO's staff. Yet even in these situations, suboptimization is still a clear and present danger if the Operator goes rogue, optimizing the business unit with a strategy formulated out of alignment with the whole-of-enterprise vision. Note that in the kind of conglomerated businesses I have run during my career, Operators have been the presidents of segments or individual operating companies. I believe that, despite the danger of suboptimization, these officers generally make the most effective Operators. They enjoy a degree of autonomy yet are constrained by their commitment to own, develop, and set the strategy within their unit *for the purpose of effectively delivering the mission goal set by the Visionary*. Successful Operators know their business unit intimately—better than anyone. Yet while they may not be experts in PGOS and 80/20, they not only grasp the principles and have a sound working knowledge of the processes, they ensure that these principles and processes, applied to their own bailiwick, serve the greater enterprise.

Operators are not the source of the overall strategy and mission, and they are not the authors of how the overall strategy is implemented. Their chief role is to put their intimate working knowledge of their units into creating a strategy for them. Having been thoroughly evangelized on the overall vision of the enterprise, they apply the 80/20 PGOS processes and practices common to the entire enterprise. This ensures that their unit seamlessly aligns with the overall strategy and contributes to meeting or exceeding enterprise-wide strategic goals.

SOME LESSONS FROM THE UNITED STATES MARINE CORPS

The Marine Corps prides itself in being the nation's elite military force: "First to arrive. Last to leave." Accordingly, the service has developed a set of leadership principles that are designed to promote autonomy and self-efficacy within a military environment in which individual action must serve a greater strategic purpose within a well-defined chain of command.

I believe that this leadership situation—striking an acute balance between independent initiative and subordination to strategic requirements—is highly instructive for Operators, who are leaders with heavy responsibilities, guided and constrained by an overall vision and strategy they do not own yet but with which they must align themselves and those they lead.

Well aware that they ask a great deal from their officers—their "operators"—the Marine Corps accordingly has formulated a detailed set of leadership principles to guide them.

MARINE LEADERSHIP PRINCIPLES

1. **Know yourself and seek self-improvement.**
   a. Evaluate yourself by using the leadership traits and determine your strengths and weaknesses.
   b. Work to improve your weaknesses and utilize your strengths.
   c. Seek the honest opinions of your friends or

superiors to show you how to improve your leadership ability.

   d. Learn by studying the causes for the success or the failure of other leaders.
   e. Master the art of effective writing and speech.

2. **Be technically and tactically proficient.**
   a. Must demonstrate the ability to accomplish the mission through competence in your MOS [Military Occupational Specialty—that is, "your job"].
   b. Seek a well-rounded military education by attending service schools; doing daily independent reading and research; taking correspondence courses from MCI [the Marine Corps Institute], colleges, or correspondence schools; and seeking off-duty education.
   c. Seek out and associate with capable leaders. Observe and study their actions.
   d. Broaden your knowledge through association with members of other branches of the U.S. armed services.
   e. Seek opportunities to apply knowledge through the exercise of command.
3. **Know your Marines and look out for their welfare.**
   a. Put your Marines' welfare before your own, correct grievances, and remove discontent.
   b. See the members of your unit and let them see you so that every Marine may know you and feel that you know them. Be approachable.

c. Help your Marines get needed support from available personal services.
d. Determine what your unit's mental attitude is; keep in touch with their thoughts.
e. Encourage individual development.
f. Provide sufficient recreational time and insist on participation.

4. **Keep your Marines informed.**
    a. Inform Marines in your unit of all happenings and give reasons why things are to be done.
    b. Whenever possible, explain why tasks must be done and how you intend to do them.
    c. Assure yourself, by frequent inspections, that immediate subordinates are passing on necessary information.
    d. Be alert to detect the spread of rumors. Stop rumors by replacing them with the truth.
    e. Build morale and esprit de corps by publicizing information concerning successes of your unit.
    f. Keep your unit informed about current legislation and regulations affecting their pay, promotion, privileges, and other benefits.
5. **Set the example.**
    a. As a Marine leader your duty is to set the standards for your Marines by personal example.
    b. Show your Marines that you are willing to do the same things you ask them to do.
    c. Be physically fit, well groomed, and correctly dressed.

d. Maintain an optimistic outlook. Develop the will to win by capitalizing on your unit's abilities. The more difficult the situation is, the better your chance is to display an attitude of calmness and confidence.
e. Conduct yourself so that your personal habits are not open to criticism.
f. Exercise initiative and promote the spirit of initiative in your Marines.
g. Avoid showing favoritism to any subordinate.
h. Share danger and hardship with your Marines to demonstrate your willingness to assume your share of the difficulties.
i. Delegate authority and avoid over-supervision in order to develop leadership among subordinates.

6. **Ensure the task is understood, supervised, and accomplished.**
   a. Communicate your instructions in a clear, concise manner.
   b. Talk at a level that your Marines are sure to understand, but not at a level so low that would insult their intelligence.
   c. Allow Marines a chance to ask questions or seek advice.
   d. Allow subordinates to use their own techniques, and then periodically check their progress.
   e. Ensure the need for an order exists before issuing the order.

f. Question your Marines to determine if there is any doubt or misunderstanding in regard to the task to be accomplished.
g. Supervise the execution of your orders.
h. Exercise care and thought in supervision. Over-supervision hurts initiative and creates resentment; under-supervision will not get the job done.

7. **Train your Marines as a team.**
   a. Train with a purpose and emphasize the essential element of teamwork.
   b. Sharing of hardships, dangers, and hard work strengthens a unit and reduces problems; it develops teamwork, improves morale and esprit, and molds a feeling of unbounded loyalty.
   c. Insist on teamwork from your Marines. Train, play, and operate as a team.
   d. Be sure that each Marine knows his/her position and responsibilities within the team framework.
   e. Never publicly blame an individual for the team's failure nor praise one individual for the team's success.
   f. Ensure that all training is meaningful, and that its purpose is clear to all members of the command.
   g. Acquaint each Marine of your unit with the capabilities and limitations of all other units, thereby developing mutual trust and understanding.

h. Base team training on realistic, current, and probable conditions.
i. Insist that every Marine understands the functions of the other members of the team and how the team functions as a part of the unit.

8. **Make sound and timely decisions.**
   a. The leader must be able to rapidly estimate a situation and make a sound decision based on that estimation.
   b. Once you make a decision and discover it is the wrong one, don't hesitate to revise your decision.
   c. Develop a logical and orderly thought process by practicing objective estimates of the situation.
   d. When time and situation permit, plan for every possible event that can reasonably be foreseen.
   e. Consider the advice and suggestions of your subordinates whenever possible before making decisions.
   f. Announce decisions in time to allow subordinates to make necessary plans.
   g. Make sure your Marines are familiar with your policies and plans.
9. **Develop a sense of responsibility among your subordinates.**
   a. Provide clear, well-thought directions. Tell your subordinates what to do, not how to do it. Hold them responsible for results, although overall responsibility remains yours. Delegate enough

authority to them to enable them to accomplish the task.

b. Give your Marines frequent opportunities to perform duties usually performed by the next higher rank.
c. Be quick to recognize your subordinates' accomplishments when they demonstrate initiative and resourcefulness.
d. Correct errors in judgment and initiative in a way which will encourage the Marine to try harder. Avoid public criticism or condemnation.
e. Give advice and assistance freely when it is requested by your subordinates.
f. Let your Marines know that you will accept honest errors without punishment in return; teach from these mistakes by critique and constructive guidance.
g. Resist the urge to micro-manage; don't give restrictive guidance which destroys initiative, drive, innovation, enthusiasm; creates boredom; and increases workload of seniors.

10. **Employ your command in accordance with its capabilities.**
    a. Seek out challenging tasks for your unit, but be sure that your unit is prepared for and has the ability to successfully complete the mission.
    b. Do not volunteer your unit for tasks it is not capable of completing.

c. Keep yourself informed as to the operational effectiveness of your command.
d. Be sure that tasks assigned to subordinates are reasonable. Do not hesitate to demand their utmost in an emergency.
e. Analyze all assigned tasks. If the means at your disposal are inadequate, inform your immediate supervisor and request the necessary support.
f. Assign tasks equally among your Marines.
g. Use the full capabilities of your unit before requesting assistance.

11. **Seek responsibility and take responsibility for your actions.**
    a. Learn the duties of your immediate senior, and be prepared to accept the responsibilities of these duties.
    b. Seek different leadership positions that will give you experience in accepting responsibility in different fields.
    c. Take every opportunity that offers increased responsibility.
    d. Perform every act, large, or small, to the best of your ability. Your reward will be increased opportunity to perform bigger and more important tasks.
    e. Stand up for what you think is right; have the courage of your convictions.
    f. Carefully evaluate a subordinate's failure before

taking action. Make sure the apparent shortcomings are not due to an error on your part. Consider the Marines that are available, salvage a Marine if possible, and replace a Marine when necessary.

g. In the absence of orders, take the initiative to perform the actions you believe your senior would direct you to perform if he/she were present.

From U.S. Marine Corps University (USMCU).

OPERATORS MAKE IT HAPPEN

The Marines have a reputation for *making it happen*. This is a concise and precise description of what an Operator must do. Those who play this role in an enterprise are the ones who make it happen. They lead their units in full alignment with the business as a whole. They transform the potential energy of vision and strategy into the kinetic energy of application and creation.

PART II

. . . AND HOW THEY USE IT

Chapter 5

DATA

"Do not seek for information of which you cannot make use."

—Anna C. Brackett, *The Technique of Rest* (1892)

Have you ever heard an executive complain about a shortage of reports? "What this company needs are more reports!" If so, you may need some pointers in recognizing sarcasm. Because nobody in the history of business has ever said it.

Digital commerce generates a lot of reports. Numbers are in its nature.

Say your digital marketing guru reports a 2% click-through rate (CTR). You are told it's twice the industry average. You are over the moon! It sounds pretty wonderful, especially the part about being *twice* the industry average. Who doesn't like to be considered twice the average?

But what, really, does a 2% click-through rate mean? What is its impact? Does a 2% CTR make a difference to *your* business? How does it move sales? Obviously, 2% is better than 1% or no percent. But does a 2% CTR move the needle? Two percent is a number. But what matters is the effect it has on another number, your sales. How does click-through translate into conversion from a couple of clicks to a sale?

Measuring CTR—or any other data—for its own sake is not a waste of time, but neither is it an indication of performance—unless, of course, you are in the click-through business. But if you are in the business of selling innovative products online, the only measurement that matters is the correlation of click-through with actual sales. If you are going to measure click-through data—and with today's software, this is very easy to do—then correlate it with sales. If you can nail the correlation, you will provide more than a measurement that satisfies curiosity. You will provide a metric for improving click-through as a *verified* means of increasing sales performance.

Measure, measure, measure. Just be certain you are measuring only data that lead to improvement. You are in the sales business, not the click-through business. Therefore, correlate click-through with sales. That *correlation* is the necessary measurement here.

Let's say that you add more data. In addition to having a CTR twice the industry average, you discover that your website traffic is up by 6% over the previous month. Moreover, your company's Google Ads are outperforming its Facebook ads. All very encouraging, but how does this correlate with sales performance?

Measure only what you can act upon to improve performance. That is, your data must be action oriented or "actionable." Otherwise, there is no business reason to collect it. The measurable data Curtis LeMay focused on was not the fact that the B-29 was a modern marvel capable of flying higher, faster, and longer than any other heavy bomber, but how efficient the aircraft was at destroying Japan's ability to continue making war. This data, quite measurable, told him that it was surprisingly ineffective in this mission. The massive tonnage of bombs, dropped from the high altitudes at which the B-29 was designed to fly, were missing their targets. So, as we saw in chapter 1, LeMay radically changed how the B-29 was being employed in the Pacific Theater.

WHAT DO *I* NEED TO KNOW?

LeMay had an existentially urgent problem. His first step was not simply to collect data, but to ask: *What do* I *need to know?* Ten years or so ago, companies invested heavily and often heedlessly in data scientists and data analytics. Today, they make similar investments in AI-driven data analytics.

Don't get me wrong, I'm a data guy. But before you invest time, effort, and money in collecting data, you need to ask and answer *What do* I *need to know?*

Back in 2013, *Harvard Business Review* published an article titled "You May Not Need Big Data After All."[1] One retailer they cited "learned that it could increase profits substantially by extending the time items were on the floor before and after discounting," only to discover that to actually do this, they would have to invest in "a complete redesign of the supply chain." The information they had was unusable. They should have understood that what they *needed to know* was data relating to actionable steps, things they could actually do.

What do I *need to know?* The *HBR* authors discovered that many companies launch costly searches for new data without doing "a good job with the information they already have. . . . They first need to learn how to use the data already embedded in their core operating systems, much the way people must master arithmetic before they tackle algebra. Until a company learns how to use data and analysis to support its operating decisions, it will not be in a position to benefit from" investing in the quest for new data, big data, or even AI-driven data.

---

1 Jeanne W. Ross, Cynthia M. Beath, and Anne Quaadgras, "You May Not Need Big Data After All," *Harvard Business Review*, December 2013, https://hbr.org/2013/12/you-may-not-need-big-data-after-all.

Figure 05-01

Peter Drucker, "father of modern management."

"What gets measured gets managed" is a tenet universally attributed to the management guru of all gurus, Peter Drucker. In fact, it likely came from V. F. Ridgway (in a 1956 paper enticingly titled "Dysfunctional Consequences of Performance Measurements") and was meant as a warning against relying too heavily on quantitative measures.[2] In other words, what gets measured gets managed, so be sure you really want or even need to manage what you are measuring. Your first question *must* be, *What do* I *need to know?*

When the PE firm I'm associated with sent me to lead a company I'll call Rolling Thunder, I came into it knowing a few things. I knew it had succeeded for decades as a $100 million company and was then sold to PE ownership, which transformed it into a $700 million company. This was data already available. So, I decided to use it by asking this question: *What could possibly be wrong with this transformation?*

As it turned out, plenty.

Rolling Thunder's growth was a good thing and a tribute to its management. Nevertheless, one piece of data had been overlooked. The company had outgrown its support systems, which had been designed and built for the original

---

2 V. F. Ridgway, "Dysfunctional Consequences of Performance Measurements," *Administrative Science Quarterly* 1, no. 2 (1956): 240–47, https://www.jstor.org/stable/2390989.

$100 million company. Because of its admirable growth, its policies and processes had become underpowered and overmatched, and the underinformed company was beginning to drift and stray from its vision and mission. Clearly, we would need to improve and right-size our policies and processes. But first, we needed to understand *where we had been* so we could understand *where we were now and how we got here.* Only with this contextual understanding could the leadership craft strategic decisions that would make tomorrow productively different from today.

Now I knew what I needed to know. I needed to ask questions about the past performance of Rolling Thunder. The answers revealed that, after the first PE firm bought the company, there had been no growth. In fact, each company that had been added to Rolling Thunder caused it to perform worse than before the conglomerate was acquired. What accounted for this?

I TOOK A 3-L TOUR

Whenever I walk into a business as its new CEO, I immediately dive into the data by taking a 3-L Tour: Listening, Learning, and then Leveraging. I'm not just talking about reading annual reports and other financials; I literally walk around the company, what students of the celebrated "Toyota Way" call doing the "Gemba Walk."

THE TOYOTA WAY AND THE GEMBA WALK

Toyota Motor Company was one of the drivers of the so-called Japanese Miracle, the nation's rapid economic recovery after its total defeat in World War II. Toyota management created an extraordinary organizational culture that was refined, improved, and ultimately promulgated in the *Toyota Production System*, issued in 2001. It became a cornerstone of lean manufacturing methodology.

Figure 05-02

Sakichi Toyoda, founder of Toyota Industries and creator of "The Toyota Production System."

The two great pillars of the Toyota Way are respect for the company's workers and a corporate ethos—practically a religion—of continuous incremental improvement. Essential to activating continuous improvement is the Gemba Walk. Executives, including the CEO, frequently walk the shop floors. They have a clear vision of what *should* be happening, and they compare it to what they see *actually* happening. They look at processes. They talk to the people who work the processes. They ask these floor-level workers what their objectives are, and they evaluate how well or poorly their objectives align with those of Toyota leadership. The gaps between the workers' understanding of their objectives and those of leadership are key data in crafting a strategy for change.

When doing a Gemba Walk, I observe what I can, and I ask the people I meet straightforward questions about the business. I ask about what's going on now, and I ask about the past, about *their* history with the company and about the history of the company itself. And then I ask people what they think the future will be—or what they want the future to be. The Gemba Walk gives me useful, real-world information.

I don't rely exclusively on casual conversation and

whatever questions occur to me. I come armed with a written questionnaire, which goes something like this:

QUESTIONS TO ASK ABOUT THE PAST

Performance

How did the company perform in the past?
How do people in the organization think it performed?
How were goals set?
Were goals realistic?
Were goals insufficiently or overly ambitious?
Were internal or external benchmarks used?
What evaluative measures were employed?
What behaviors did they encourage and discourage?
What were the consequences if goals were not met?

Root Causes

If past performance was good, why? If poor, why?
How did the company's strategy, structure, technical capabilities, culture, and politics impact performance?

History of Change

What efforts have been made to change the company and what were the results?
Who was most instrumental in shaping this organization?

QUESTIONS TO ASK ABOUT THE PRESENT

Strategy

What is the stated vision/strategy of the company?

Is the company genuinely pursuing the stated vision/strategy? If no, why? If yes, is the strategy likely to take the organization where it needs to go?

People

Who is capable and who is not?

Who is trustworthy and who is not?

Who are the influencers and why?

Processes

What are the key processes of the organization?

Are they effective? If not, why not?

Dangers

What dangers lurk? Booby traps?

Early Wins

Where can you achieve some early wins?

QUESTIONS ABOUT THE FUTURE

Challenges and Opportunities

What areas pose the greatest challenges next year? (Can anything be done now to prepare for them?)

What are the most promising unexploited opportunities? (How can they be realized?)

Barriers and Resources

What are the highest barriers to needed change?

What high-quality resources can be leveraged?

What new capabilities need to be developed or acquired?

Culture

What cultural changes need to be preserved or nurtured?

What cultural changes need to be changed?

What are the most promising unexploited growth opportunities?

Ask stakeholders: "If you were me, where would you focus your attention?"

The reason for preparing a questionnaire is to save time by ensuring that you ask the questions to which *you* really want answers. It is a way to elicit from people at all levels in the company the data you believe will enable you to drive productive change. If you've never run across a book by

Atul Gawande called *The Checklist Manifesto,* I recommend you look it up and buy it. As Gawande explains, checklists are "among the basic tools of . . . quality and productivity," especially in fields "combining high risk and complexity." Gawande points out that checklists may "seem lowly and simplistic, but they help fill in for the gaps in our brains and between our brains."

Arming yourself with a questionnaire or a checklist of questions primes your mind to pick up on relevant strengths and weaknesses. It will also challenge your assumptions, either confirming or refuting them. An incoming CEO must assume that, in the words of *X-Files*' Agent Fox Mulder, "The answer is out there." You must always assume the answers are out there. Just ask the right people. If you don't know who the right people are, ask whomever you can. Even if they may be the wrong people, they should be able to suggest somebody who does have the answers. The failure to get answers usually begins with a failure to ask questions. This is obvious, but no less true for it.

On my Gemba Walk, I identified the right people to ask, and I asked them. What I discovered was that the company had limped along for quite some time with an absentee CEO—the son of the founder—who spent most of his time away from the company. He did have a "strategy," however, which consisted of one goal: acquisition. This explained why the operational leadership of the conglomerate company lacked alignment. The company's previous owner removed that CEO but was unable to replace him for some eighteen months. During this time, the business drifted. When I was hired, many of the company's problems were obvious, but you must not assume that the problems you can see are the only problems. Nevertheless, you must act first on the obvious. If the boat is leaking, plug the holes. If the house is burning, douse the flames. And then go about finding the rest of the answers.

My 3-L Tours combine spontaneous employee conversations with their answers to my questionnaire. My first questions are always very direct—basically, "What's happening?" and "How's the business? What's working? What's not working? Hey, tell me what you like about your job, what you don't. What's going right and wrong?" I also set up a series of three one-on-one meetings with key managers.

MEETING 1: GETTING ACQUAINTED

Getting to know each other on a personal level

Things I would like to know:

1. Tell me about your work and your role. What skills do you bring to your role?
2. What are the most rewarding aspects of your job?

3. Why do you do your job, besides for the paycheck?
4. How can I support you?
5. What brings out the best in you? What are your work preferences and styles?
6. How would you describe the business and what's working or not working?
7. What are you most proud of in this past year? Why?
8. What do you like to do when you're not working?
9. If you could make a request of anyone in the company, what would you ask for? Why?

Potential topics you might like to share:

1. What I would like Bill to know about me is . . .
2. I would describe my own leadership style as . . .
3. What excites me most about my role is . . .
4. My single greatest concern is . . .
5. The two things that would help us be more successful are . . .
6. To get the most out of my performance, it helps to . . .

7. What requires our immediate attention is . . .
8. I consider your (Bill's) top three priorities to be . . .

Feel free to ask me any questions.

I take time to digest the first meeting—in other words, to really get acquainted. When I feel ready, I set up the second set of one-on-one meetings, which are devoted to "Discussing the Business":

MEETING 2: DISCUSSING THE BUSINESS

Let's talk about the business and your role

Topics that will help me learn how the organization works:

1. Business performance: Objectives, Goals, Strategies, Tactics, Financials
2. People and Team: How are things working in your area? How do we engage our people? Who are our high performers? What is the level of engagement?

3. Customers: What do customers say about our products? What challenges are we facing in the market?
4. Distributors, Vendors, and Partnerships: What is our strategy for working with others? Who are considered our strategic partners?
5. Working Together: Roles and Expectations
6. Processes: How are the processes enabling or hindering work outputs?
7. Working Across the Organization: How do you and your team work with other areas?
8. Opportunities and Challenges: Give examples.
9. Support: What support do you need from me, and what other resource requirements do you have?
10. Professional Career Development: What are your career aspirations?
11. Miscellaneous: What other advice do you have as we move forward?

We may not have time to cover all subjects in this meeting. I am looking for a high-level overview that will enable us to delve into more detailed discussion in the future.

Again, I take the time to study my notes from this meeting before setting up the third round, which is a "Deeper Dive Business Review":

MEETING 3: DEEPER DIVE BUSINESS REVIEW

This is an opportunity to validate and confirm knowledge about the business and to seek input on next steps. It builds on Meeting 2 and emphasizes:

1. Key initiatives in which the manager to whom you are speaking is involved
2. Opportunities and challenges for all parties
3. Risks the company faces
4. Resource requirements
5. Process or system requirements
6. A review of the talent on the manager's team

PRIORITIZE

If your house is on fire, douse the flames. If your boat is sinking, plug the leaks. No-brainers, right? Most of us would describe these existential issues as urgent—life or death.

We'd be only half right.

Few people have had more responsibility heaped upon them than General Dwight D. Eisenhower, who was named Supreme Allied Commander, Europe, during World War II. Daily—hourly—he was bombarded by crises, problems, and opportunities. What we would call urgent—lives depending on it—he further defined on *two* axes, urgency *and* importance. Only matters that were both *urgent and important* took precedence over everything else and were addressed immediately (those in Quad A; see figure 05-03).

If you are in charge, the responsibility for doing what needs to be done in cases of combined urgency and importance is *yours.*

Some things are *important but not urgent.* They need to be done, but not before those that are both *urgent and important.* If *urgent and important* deserves to be put into Quad A, *important but not urgent* merits Quad B. As Eisenhower saw it, perhaps surprisingly, Quad C held matters that are *urgent but not important.* These could be delegated or automated. If neither alternative is available, you yourself could attend to Quad C tasks but only after addressing the tasks in Quad A. Finally, if a thing is *neither important nor urgent*, ignore and avoid it by tossing it into Quad D.

	Urgent	Not Urgent
Important	A (Manage) • Crisis • Medical emergencies • Pressing problems • Deadline-driven projects • Last-minute preparations for scheduled activities	B (Focus) • Preparation/planning • Prevention • Values clarification • Exercise • Relationship-building • True recreation/relaxation
	Quadrant of Necessity	**Quadrant of Quality & Personal Leadership**
Not Important	C (Avoid) • Interruptions, some calls • Some mail & reports • Some meetings • Many "pressing" matters • Many popular activities	D (Avoid) • Trivia, busywork • Junk mail • Some phone messages/email • Time wasters • Escape activities • Viewing mindless TV shows
	Quadrant of Deception	**Quadrant of Waste**

Figure 05-03

The "Eisenhower Matrix."

To apply this matrix to your own work, first identify your Bucket A (important and urgent) priorities. Within this category, the topmost priority is any existential (immediate life-and-death) issues. But do not necessarily limit your A priorities to these. Also look for items that are easy wins. Nothing is more inspirational and morale boosting within an organization than scoring early triumphs. These do more than make people feel good; they bolster or even create what psychologists call "self-efficacy," the belief that you have the knowledge, skill, and competence to solve your problems, leverage your opportunities, and perform your assigned missions. The earlier you generate a mindset of self-efficacy within your organization by scoring easy, early wins, the sooner you will build the emotional and mindset momentum that is critical in driving the business to achieve all its strategic goals.

Generally speaking, Bucket A priorities exhibit the following characteristics:

1. They flow from fundamental problems.
2. They are specific rather than vague or general.
3. They suggest a clear direction but also allow for flexibility, so that actions can be modified as necessary to suit a changing situation or fresh information and data about the current and evolving situation.

You can distill the Eisenhower Matrix to a single key principle: *Focus on what is important, in both the urgent and the nonurgent categories. Avoid everything else.* But also reflect on the nature of urgent problems:

1. They demand attention because the consequences of not addressing them are usually serious, sinister, and immediate.
2. Understand that *urgent* issues are almost always imposed on you. That is, they reflect somebody else's goals.

3. In contrast to most *urgent* issues, *important* issues are key to achieving *your* goals, *your* strategic ends, even if their consequences are less immediate.

Begin by distinguishing the important from the unimportant. Set the unimportant aside. Note that both the *urgent important* and the *nonurgent important* are *important*. For practical, existential reasons, you must address the *urgent important* first. But attend to the *nonurgent important* as soon as possible. Once you determine what is both important *and* urgent, you can focus on these issues and reserve sufficient time and resources to turn, as soon as possible, to the *nonurgent important*.

CONVERT DATA INTO IMPROVEMENT WITH 80/20

In *The Signal and the Noise: Why So Many Predictions Fail—but Some Don't*, an important book from 2012, predictive statistician Nate Silver uses a concept that radio and audio engineers developed many years earlier. S/N, the signal-to-noise ratio, is used to compare the level of desired *signal* (reproduced or transmitted music, for instance, or speech) versus the level of background *noise* (static, for example, or hiss), which obscures the signal. Statisticians like Silver use the concept of S/N to discuss the ratio of the power of meaningful data input (the signal) to the power of meaningless or irrelevant data input (the noise).

We have discussed some ways of separating the signal from the noise in choosing what data to gather and analyze for improving or turning around a business:

1. You can study the history and present state of the business based on standard business documents and reports, and on talking to employees at various levels in the business (doing the Gemba Walk).
2. You can determine what issues—problems, challenges, and opportunities—are both *important and urgent*, are *important but not urgent*, are *urgent but not important*, and are *neither urgent nor important.*
3. You can distinguish, first, between data that is measurable (and thus potentially *signal*) and data that cannot be measured (and is therefore *noise*).
4. Of the data capable of being measured, you should measure only what can be improved.

We can further refine #3 and #4. I would dismiss as *noise* all data that is incapable of guiding improvement. Only what can be both measured *and* improved is valuable as *signal*, information useful and capable of being acted upon.

If you want tomorrow to be different from today, do something different today. The question is: What should that "something" be? The answer is found by applying the 80/20 Rule, which shows you precisely what to do "different."

Here's how.

Some mathematical ratios appear to have mystical powers

or, at the very least, hold the key to powerful relationships in nature and beyond. In 2002, Mario Livio, an Israeli American physicist, wrote a book called *The Golden Ratio: The Story of Phi, the World's Most Astonishing Number.* It's all about a certain irrational number (a number that cannot be expressed as the ratio of two integers), often shortened to 1.618, called phi (φ). This number, φ, denotes what ancient Greek mathematicians called the Golden Ratio, an instance in which the ratio of two quantities (*a* and *b*) is the same as the ratio of their sum (*a* + *b*) to the larger of the two quantities. Livio wrote:

> Some of the greatest mathematical minds of all ages from Pythagoras and Euclid in Greece, through the medieval Italian mathematician Leonardo of Pisa and the Renaissance astronomer Johannes Kepler, to present-day scientific figures such as Oxford physicist Roger Penrose, have spent endless hours over this simple ratio. Biologists, artists, musicians, historians, architects, psychologists, and even mystics have pondered and debated the basis of its ubiquity and appeal. In fact, it is probably fair to say that the Golden Ratio has inspired thinkers of all disciplines like no other number in the history of mathematics.

Check it out: The Golden Ratio governs the number of petals in a flower, determines the spiral pattern in seed heads (just picture the center of a sunflower), governs the seed pod arrangement of pinecones, explains the way tree branches form or split, determines the structure of spiral shells (such as the nautilus), perfectly describes the structure of spiral galaxies, applies accurately to the structure of hurricanes, explains the relationship of the features of the human face to one another, accounts for the fact that the length of each section of our fingers is larger than the preceding one by φ, describes the proportions of human and animal bodies, forms the flight pattern of birds of prey as they spiral down on their targets, and describes the structure of the DNA molecule.

Figure 05-04

Snail shells whose growth factor is φ develop according to the logarithmic spiral commonly known as the Golden Ratio. Like the Pareto Principle, the Golden Ratio is a natural law.

I can't tell you why the Golden Ratio is golden, but I can tell you that, in its way, the Pareto Principle—the 80/20 ratio—is golden, too. Like the classical Golden Ratio, 80/20 applies to a dazzling array of disparate phenomena in virtually all areas of nature and human endeavor. Recognition of 80/20 started when the Italian polymath Vilfredo Pareto (1848–1923) discovered that 80% of the peapods in his garden were produced by just 20% of his pea plants and, conversely, just 20% of his pea plants produced 80% of his viable peapods.

Interesting. But is this seemingly random observation a quirk or a law of nature? In other words, is it noise, or is it signal?

Pareto spent years investigating his pea plant observation and discovered that in every system of any kind he looked into, 20% of input is responsible for 80% of productive output, whereas the other 80% of the input is essentially wasted on unproductive results. Pareto's 80/20 Principle is a rule—in fact, I believe it deserves to be called a law of nature. More to the point for those of us in business, it is a breakthrough because it tells us that any for-profit enterprise generates 80% of its revenue from the combination of just 20% of its customers buying just 20% of its products. The non-mathematical name for these two groups is "my best customers" and "my best products."

But also take a hard look at yourself. If you could do a close auditing of your workdays, you would discover that 80% of what you achieve in a given workday is the product of 20% of your time. Sounds good until you realize that this also means that 80% of your daily minutes and hours result in trivialities.

It should come as no surprise that successful CEOs and managers use 80/20 to design businesses that focus 80% of their resources on serving the 20% of customers who generate 80% of their gross sales. Because it is possible—indeed, pretty easy—to track the numbers, you can soon discover which customers buying which products are your "80s," the customers and products responsible for 80% of your gross sales. (As we will see later in this book, this 80% of gross revenue produces something like 200% of your profits.)

For ancient Greek artists and architects, there was no intuition or guesswork involved in creating a sculpture or temple according to the Golden Ratio. For the same reason, you don't have to await a flash of genius to apply the Pareto Principle. Gather the data, work the numbers, and act on the result of the analysis.

You can apply 80/20 to virtually every aspect of your business: HR headcount, task and process planning, customers, markets, products, and processes. It will guide you away from wasting or otherwise suboptimally misallocating resources. 80/20 offers a clear-cut tool for distinguishing the critical few from the trivial many and deploying your precious resources to serve (actually, to purposely overserve) the former while reducing resources allocated to the latter. Instead of doing what Vilfredo Pareto observed that we human beings normally do—namely, expend 80% of whatever we have for a pitiful 20% gain—we can use the 80/20 Rule to stop diverting resources from the critical to the trivial. The 80/20 Rule is the engine that drives what I call the Profitable

Growth Operating System (PGOS), essentially a systematic means of applying Pareto's observation.

GET INTO THE HABIT OF THINKING OF "SEGMENT" AS A VERB

So much in life is about separating the wheat from the chaff, the nourishment from the empty calories. A PGOS business applying 80/20 does this by segmenting its customers and products to reveal how it can devote as much as 80% of its resources to the 20% of products and customers that are most productive.

Segmenting is the first step toward leading the company strategy through the 80/20 process. Begin by collecting the necessary data. For each *product*, record total sales, number of customers who purchased the product, and the gross margin this has produced over the quarter just ended. Then, record the total sales for each *customer*. Having done this, analyze the data. The simplest way to go about this follows:

1. List your products in descending order of their sales, from highest to lowest.
2. Now, list your customers in descending order by total sales, from most dollars to fewest.
3. Last, segment your products and customers by identifying the top 20% of each. Take your lists and draw a line between 20% and 21%. The products

> and customers above the line are, by absolute 80/20 definition, the critical few. The rest, also by definition, are the trivial many.

Segmenting by 80/20 is a big step in the right direction. The segmented lists separate the critical few from the trivial many. You now have two lists, one consisting of your top-performing products, the other of your top-performing customers—with "top-performing" defined as the 20% responsible for 80% of your gross revenue.

So, now you know a lot. But you still need to transform that information into something actionable in order to produce the improvement specifically known as growth. To make this transformation, you need to know how the product data intersects with the customer data.

On its face, the Pareto Principle sounds pretty gloomy: 80% of what you do or invest yields just 20% of your revenue. You might feel doomed to mostly be unproductive . . . but not if you counter the doom with strategic growth.

Growth is not free. It is earned. To earn the right to grow, you've got to do a lot better than surrender to the 80/20 Rule. Instead, you must fashion this Law of Uneven Distribution into an engine of growth by creating a strategy to more efficiently deploy your resources to chiefly serve (overserve) the combination of high-performing products and high-performing customers. To do this, locate the intersection of product data and customer data, because looking only at products provides a partial and therefore distorted picture of what your key customers (call them your A customers) are buying from you. Earning the right to grow demands understanding more than the cumulative sales of products. You must have a picture of your customers' needs and wants as they are made manifest in the total basket of products they buy from you. At the same time, focusing exclusively on your customers will lead you to miss why different customers end up in different quadrants. If you can see the *intersection* of products and customers, you can discover patterns in customer behavior that will guide the strategic design of your systems and processes.

To create a picture capable of driving an effective analysis, you need more than a simple two-way 80/20 division. You need a map—a chart divided into quadrants to show you the four corners of the 80/20 customer/product alignments. (In practice, both the quadrants and the chart they make up are called "quads.") Label your top-performing customers (the top 20%) "A customers" and the rest (the lower 80%) "B customers." Label your top-performing products (the top 20%) "A products" and the rest (the lower 80%) "B products." Now combine customers with the products they buy and calculate the percentage each quad contributes to total sales:

Quad 1 consists of A customers buying A products (0.8 × 0.8) = 64% of sales

Quad 2 consists of A customers buying B products (0.8 × 0.2) = 16% of sales

Quad 3 consists of B customers buying A products (0.2 × 0.8) = 16% of sales

Quad 4 consists of B customers buying B products (0.2 × 0.2) = 4% of sales
Total Sales = 100%

When you combine customers with the products they buy, the 80/20 ratio is not clearly visible on the surface, but it is nevertheless in the math. The combination of A customers and A products is 80% (0.8) times 80% (0.8), which is 64% of sales, and so on through the rest of the possible combinations. Figure 05-05 shows the graphic representation:

QUAD 1: A customers/A products 0.8 × 0.8 = 64% of sales	QUAD 2: A customers/B products 0.8 × 0.2 = 16% of sales
QUAD 3: B customers/A products 0.2 × 0.8 = 16% of sales	QUAD 4: B customers/B products 0.2 × 0.2 = 4% of sales

Figure 05-05

The 80/20 Quad template.

Now that you have a template for dealing productively with your data, the next chapter will show you how to use the template to apply 80/20 to the real world.

Chapter 6

ANALYSIS

> "Given for one instant an intelligence which could comprehend all the forces by which nature is animated and the respective positions of the beings which compose it, if moreover this intelligence were vast enough to submit these data to analysis, it would embrace in the same formula both the movements of the largest bodies in the universe and those of the lightest atom; to it nothing would be uncertain, and the future and past would be present to its eyes."
>
> —Pierre Simon Laplace,
> *Théorie analytique des probabilités*

By now you know how I feel about 80/20, the Pareto Principle. It is a law of nature and can take its place beside any other set of natural laws. Take Newton's Three Laws of Motion.

First Law

Objects in motion tend to stay in motion, and objects at rest tend to stay at rest unless an outside force acts upon them.

Second Law

The rate of change of the momentum of a body is directly proportional to the net force acting on it, and the direction of the change in momentum takes place in the direction of the net force.

Third Law

To every action (force applied) there is an equal but opposite reaction (equal force applied in the opposite direction).

As natural laws, Newton's laws and the Pareto Principle both serve two purposes. They *describe* aspects of the behavior of nature. This is valuable and interesting, but understanding these various behaviors provides a second benefit. It tells us how we can manipulate or manage aspects of natural behavior to accomplish certain goals.

For instance, if you want your car to stop, you need an outside force to act upon it (First Law). This force needs to be sufficient to change the vehicle's momentum (Second Law). So, in designing a set of brakes, you must calculate the net force that the engine and transmission produce together and design a braking system capable of a net force greater than this. At the same time, you likely need to take into account certain Third Law data, particularly the coefficient of friction that applies to the forward motion the vehicle creates by the rotation of the wheels where they contact the road. Think of slippery versus dry conditions, for example.

My point is that natural laws are both *descriptive* and *prescriptive*, whether you are pondering Newton's Three Laws of Motion or the Pareto Principle of 80/20. Moving from the description to the prescription requires analysis. It is the analysis that sets you up for change, whether it is knowing how to design more effective brakes or how to turn your company around and position it for growth.

The Rule of 3 will get you there, but it is a fixed menu and not a buffet. All three roles—the Visionary, the Prophet(s), and the Operators—are required and must be fully aligned on the data, what it means, and what it drives. The Visionary is both the first and the final decision maker. Functioning from a deep, data-based understanding of both the past and present state of the enterprise, the Visionary sets a goal and envisions a plan for the desired future state the goal represents. As important as these functions are, they cannot succeed unless the Visionary secures complete alignment with the Prophet(s) and the Operators.

Prophet(s) must be the faithful keepers, interpreters, and evangelists of the vision, ministering to the organization's Operators—the leaders and managers who run the ground-level workings of the business within subsidiary companies, business units, and divisions. Operators must be accountable for implementing and executing the strategy within their domains.

It is a grave mistake to think of Operators as cogs in a wheel. On the contrary, they are positioned to understand their segments, units, or companies intimately. They should be leveraged as a source of ideas and innovation. While the Operators' input must serve the overall strategy, it should also contribute to the continuous improvement of its execution. Their on-the-ground perspective positions them to deliver detailed feedback on the performance of processes, initiatives, and changes.

SIMPLE GIFTS

The United Society of Believers in Christ's Second Appearing, better known as the Shakers, was founded in England in 1747. Shortly before the American Revolution, some Shakers sailed to America and eventually established nineteen separate communities in the Northeast, Ohio, and Kentucky. One of their religious practices undermined the longevity of the Shaker movement: They did not believe in procreation, depending instead on adoption and conversion of recruits for their perpetuation. By 1984, the year the prolific American filmmaker Ken Burns released his *Shakers* documentary, just a handful of the faithful were still alive, living in a small settlement in Maine.

Figure 06-01

"Shakers near Lebanon, state of N. York, their mode of worship" is an 1830 woodcut. "Simplicity" was a key Shaker value and religion precept.

Tiny as it was, this sect left a bright place in American memory. Some Shakers produced beautifully simple, elegant, and practical furniture. The "Shaker Style" is widely imitated to this day. The Shakers also left a musical tradition, including a hymn called "Simple Gifts." Written in 1848 by a Shaker elder (likely Joseph Brackett of the Shaker community in Alfred, Maine), the tune and its lyrics have survived, and many of us have heard it in the version composer Aaron Copland created for his famous *Appalachian Spring* (1944) and his *Old American Songs* (1950). The lyrics are contained in a single stanza:

'Tis the gift to be simple, 'tis the gift to be free
'Tis the gift to come down where we ought to be,
And when we find ourselves in the place just right,
'Twill be in the valley of love and delight.
When true simplicity is gained,
To bow and to bend we shan't be ashamed,
To turn, turn will be our delight,
Till by turning, turning we come 'round right.

For the Shakers, living simply was a goal for living well. They sought simplification as the path to the "freedom" and "delight" that comes from living "just right." This lyric, I believe, has much to teach us about leading an enterprise, which is, after all, a community of people dedicated to achieving growth in their business, their welfare, their lives, and, very often, their larger community, their nation, and even their world. To achieve all these admirable things requires simplification.

For even the largest and most complex business endeavors, it is a gift to be simple, a gift to be free from wasteful distraction and detour, and a gift to "come down where we ought to be." Pareto's 80/20 Principle is, above all, a principle of simplification.

80/20 is your GPS to a place called Simplification. Unlike some GPS units, it won't drive the car for you. It will just advise you which way to turn and when. Most importantly, 80/20 will not tell you to fire a brigade of people or randomly toss out a tranche of product lines. You cannot simply fire and cut your way to growth. Growth is a *strategic* goal. The most important fact this implies is the existence of a *strategy* for growth. Simplification is focusing and cutting with the strategic purpose of growth.

80/20 analysis will identify the customers and the products they buy that make the greatest impact on your business for good (profit) and bad (loss). It identifies them by segmenting them. The two main segments are the 20% of the intersection of your customers and products that produce 80% of your gross revenue. (That is, 80% of your revenue comes from 20% of your customers, who are in the top 20% because they buy the top 20% of your products.) Another way to look at this is that 100% of your company's input (investment in products, personnel, and costs to acquire customers) yields just 20% of your gross revenue. This means that 80% of your input is pretty close to wasted. If you are a glass-half-full type, you might want to say that just 20% of your effort is critical to your success. The rest—80%—is allocated to trivial activity, work that either fails to build revenue or actually costs you money.

Newton's First Law of Motion, which says (in part) that *objects in motion tend to stay in motion . . . unless an outside force acts upon them*, does not doom you to crash your car into a wall. It implies that you *could* do just that, if you fail to strategically (that is, purposefully) apply an outside force either to alter the direction of travel or to stop whatever is driving the forward motion. Similarly, the Pareto

Principle does not doom you to waste 80% of your input on the *trivial* and settle for a measly 20% of output that is *critical*. On the contrary, 80/20 analysis lets you know loud and clear that it would be to your great advantage to reallocate resources from the misspent 80% not merely to serve but to overserve the critical 20% of your customers and products.

What comprises simplification?

Mainly, it's about paring down "complexity"—that is, the sources of any outlays (excluding overhead) that exceed the revenue they produce. So, simplification may call for reducing the number of products, colors, or models in a given product line. Jettison the losers. Retain the winners. This is the basis of simplification. (There are alternatives to simplification, the most common of which is pricing up an ailing item to a point where it no longer books a loss or just breaks even, but actually makes a profit. We will have more to say about this in chapter 7.)

When you simplify your product line, you will likely lose some customers. You should view this loss as strategically simplifying your customer base. Common sense tells us that a successful business focuses on *expanding*, not *shrinking*, its customer base. A corollary to this commonsense assumption is that losing a customer is always bad. In fact, there is nothing good about selling a product that results in a loss. Fix this poisonous situation by either charging more for the product or dropping it altogether. Either way, you may lose a customer. But if serving that customer causes you to lose money, you don't want that customer or the product they're buying.

Simplifying your product lines necessarily simplifies your customer base. There are other ways to simplify your customer base, including reducing the geographical reach of the business and its sales territory, and reducing the number of products and product categories that require the extensive involvement of sales personnel, account executives, support staff, and so on. Investing significantly in consultative selling for the top 20% of products that generate 80% of your revenue might make sense, but it makes no sense to fund this kind of selling for products that account for the remaining 20% of your revenue.

Simplification is not *simply* about cutting costs. It is also very much about strategically allocating resources and their cost. It is highly unlikely that you will find success by firing 80% of your sales and service employees and retaining only the 20% who are top performers. It is also highly unlikely that you will find success by dropping 80% of your SKUs. The strategic choice is to reallocate as many of your top sales and service personnel to overserve and overresource your top-20% customers. And, as you are soon to see, there are ways to reallocate resources to deliver excellent service to customers on the perimeter of the top 20%. Overresource customers on this second tier, and you may be able to promote them to the top tier—that is, incentivize them to buy more, through top-tier customer service.

Many executives are more inclined to "streamline

operations" by reducing personnel rather than cutting product lines or shedding customers, even those products and customers that are unproductive. To bolster this position, these leaders may cite the late, great management guru Peter Drucker, who once declared that the "purpose of business is to create and keep a customer." This, of course, is 180 degrees from the proposition that the purpose of business is to lose a customer. But these executives should rummage around in their business school notes until they find where Drucker also concluded that most companies produce too many products in too great variety, and that they are overeager to expand into markets and economic sectors they would be better off avoiding. There is a strategic way to amend Drucker while still honoring the essence of his insight. We can say: *Business has two purposes: (1) to create and keep customers who produce profit while shedding those who produce only costs and (2) to make and sell products that create and keep profitable customers while discontinuing those products that produce nothing but costs.*

APPLYING 80/20

For a Visionary, 20/20 vision is not a good thing. To lead a business to profitable growth requires 80/20 vision, as Vilfredo Pareto saw the world. Such seeing is a faculty of data-based perception, analysis, and judgment built on the natural Law of Uneven Distribution. Pareto observed that a dramatically wide range of distributions—in the biological world, in the physical world, and in the world of human activity, including labor (work or effort), business, economics, politics, and society—were demonstrably governed by an 80/20 ratio. Specifically, approximately 80% of consequences come from about 20% of causes.

Statisticians classify the Law of Uneven Distribution (including the Pareto Principle) as a "Power Law," one that describes a functional relationship between two values or quantities, in which a change in one value creates a relative change in the other that is proportional to a power (mathematical exponent) of the other value. This sounds more obscure than it is, so the following example will draw you a picture.

Imagine a square (A). To compute the area of A, you simply calculate the square of one side (a^2). If a side measures 3 inches, say, the area of the square is $3^2 = 9$ square inches. If you double the length of the sides (to 6 inches), the area is multiplied by a factor of 4: 9 square inches × 4 = 36 square inches. You can prove this by calculating 6^2: 36 square inches. The area of the square (quantity A) varies as a power of a side (quantity a^2). The magnitude of the change created in the area of a square by doubling a side will always be a factor of 4.

Pareto showed that approximately 80% of consequences come from 20% of causes. Plot this out, and you get a Power Law Graph.

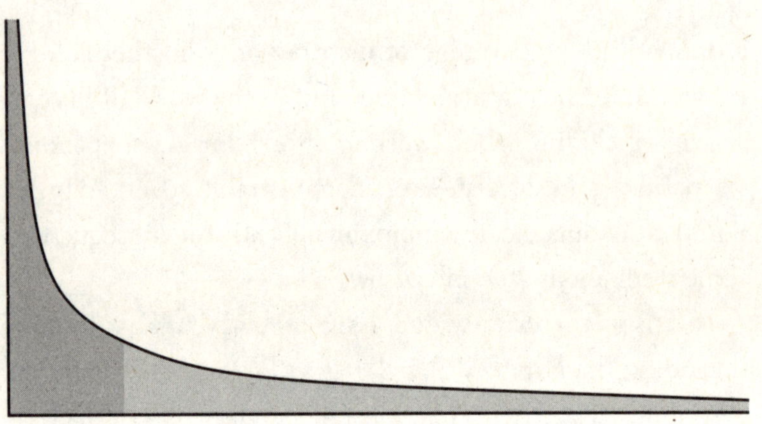

Figure 06-02

This "power curve" illustrates 80/20 distribution. The portion at left is the "critical" 20%. To the right of it is the "trivial" 80%.

The shaded area to the left is the ~20% of causes that create ~80% of consequences. The rest of the curve (to the right) is the ~80% of causes that create ~20% of consequences. Put in business terms, the shaded area is the ~20% of your customers (by definition, your best customers) who buy ~20% of your products (by definition, your best products) that create ~80% of your revenue. The rest of the curve is the ~80% of your customers who buy the ~80% of your products that create only ~20% of your revenue.

The Power-Law Curve looks dismal because the notion that 80% of your effort and investment produces just 20% of your revenue and is thus "trivial" *is* dismal. If you are a glass-half-full person, you might dispel the gloom by contemplating that a mere 20% of your effort and investment produces 80% of your revenue and is therefore "critical" or "vital." Indeed, the Pareto Principle is often called the Law of the Critical (or Vital) Few and the Trivial Many.

Fortunately, you do not have to contemplate the Curve in despair or console yourself with just 20% satisfaction. Remember, we humans have learned to understand the laws of nature and, often, use them to our advantage. So, if about 80% of what you do produces trivial results, why not figure out a way to stop doing that 80%—or at least cut back on it—and concentrate instead on doing more with the 20% that produces "critical" or "vital" results?

80/20 and the underlying fact of uneven distribution are mathematical descriptions of the world, much like the laws of physics. It is the job of the Visionary to gain insight from these laws and to use this 80/20 insight to rethink and reshape how the business invests its precious time, effort, and material resources to eliminate or reduce outlays on the trivial many in the 80%, while transforming some portion of this underproductive business segment into something better. This is the essence of turnaround leadership.

An effective Visionary sees everything through 80/20 glasses. Uneven distribution applies to work, workers, markets, customers, products—every aspect of the enterprise. This can seem overwhelming, but it also presents an overwhelmingly rich array of opportunities for improvement. Be neither discouraged nor intimidated. Successful Visionaries are those who wield 80/20 as their most powerful tool. It presents an opportunity to leverage a natural law toward better understanding the business and optimizing performance.

Strategy creates the actions required to turn the uneven distribution of input and output to the advantage of the enterprise.

Successful Visionaries understand that the Pareto Principle points the way toward competitive advantages that create profitable growth. This being the case, they also understand the critical importance of ensuring that the Prophet(s) and Operators are thoroughly versed in 80/20 analysis and are committed to being guided by it in perfect alignment. This knowledge and alignment are so critically important that the Visionary condition the employment of the Prophet(s) and Operators on championing 80/20 processes. Questions and ideas for improvement are always welcome, but they must embrace the orthodoxy of this core alignment.

MEASURE ONLY WHAT CAN BE IMPROVED

Having too little data is obviously a problem, but is it possible to collect too much data? In a word, yes.

Obtaining data from any dynamic enterprise—and few human activities are more dynamic than business—is important, but what you most urgently need is the information necessary for steering the business. Put another way: Measure and report only what is capable of being improved. This means you will want data on sales, revenue, margin, and the performance of employees, customers, markets, products, and processes. All these categories are subject to improvement.

Don't even try to swallow and digest data whole. This can only produce heartburn or worse. Instead, *segment* your customer data and product data to position your business to devote as much as 80% of its resources to your most productive products and customers.

Obtain the transaction data (typically) for a full year, collecting information on revenue, cost, quantity, who bought what—every purchase order, every line item. You need to identify the strategic intersection of the customers and their products as shown in the transaction data. Take this data and arrange it in the strategic relationship that is the 80/20 Quad Analysis (see the sample business analysis in figure 06-03).

1. Start with the box at the upper left. This is Quad 1, the customers and the products they buy that yield 80% of the revenue. These customers and products are called "the 80s." It is the intersection of A customers and A products (AA).
2. Per Pareto's observation, this group of customers constitutes roughly 20% of the company's customers buying roughly 20% of the company's products, the top customers buying the top products.
3. The rest of the customers and products they buy are roughly 80% of the customers and 80% of the

products they buy, which produce roughly 20% of the company's revenue. These customers and products are called "the 20s." They aren't all created equal, however, and can be distributed over Quads 2 through 4.

4. Quad 2 is the intersection of A customers and the B products they buy (AB). The customers in this quad are members of the 80s (the 20% responsible for 80% of revenue) but they buy products that are among the 80% of products that produce only 20% of revenue.
5. Quad 3 is the intersection of B customers and A products (BA). While these customers are members of the group that produces only 20% of revenue, some also buy A products, the products in the group that produce 80% of revenue.
6. Quad 4 is the intersection of B customers and B products (BB). This intersection contains members of both the 80% of low-performing customers and the 80% of low-performing products.

To sum up at this point, Quad 1 contains the high-volume customers who buy high-volume products; Quad 2 contains high-volume customers who buy low-volume products; Quad 3 contains low-volume customers who buy high-volume products; and Quad 4 contains low-volume customers who buy low-volume products.

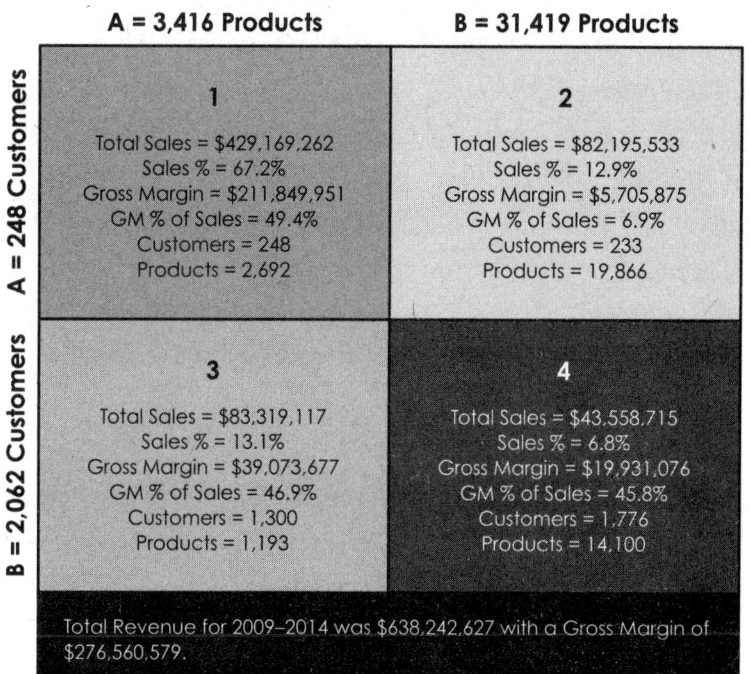

Figure 06-03

Sample 80/20 Quad chart, with underperforming Quad 4 as a candidate for extensive simplification or even dropping.

The 80/20 Rule tells us that 80% of output is produced by just 20% of input. In the context of business, this translates to 80% of sales being produced by the 20% of customers (by definition, your top-performing customers) who buy 80% of your top-performing products, which are roughly 20% of your total products. On the downside, the remaining 80% of customers produce just 20% of sales. Thus, 80/20 predicts the following, which is precisely what we saw in figure 05-05.

Quad 1: A customers buying A products (0.8 × 0.8) = 64% of sales

Quad 2: A customers buying B products (0.8 × 0.2) = 16% of sales

Quad 3: B customers buying A products (0.2 × 0.8) = 16% of sales

Quad 4: B customers buying B products (0.2 × 0.2) = 4% of sales

Total Sales = 100%

Reality, as reflected in figure 06-03, obviously varies from the 80/20 prediction presented in chapter 5. Here is the reality derived from a real-life example:

Quad 1 sales: 67.2% (actual) vs. 64% (predicted)
Quad 2 sales: 12.9% (actual) vs. 16% (predicted)
Quad 3 sales: 13.1% (actual) vs. 16% (predicted)
Quad 4 sales: 6.8% (actual) vs. 4% (predicted)

Does the variance between actual sales and predicted sales disprove 80/20 as a natural law? No. Not at all.

To begin with, because the quad chart puts together the separate customer and product quartiles—by definition four equal 25% slices of the pie—a variance from the theoretical 80/20 division is already introduced. More important, however, is that the 80/20 prediction is to the 80/20 reality what the MPG number on the window of your new gas-powered car (or "MPG equivalent" of your new EV) is to the individual driver's MPG results. The small type on the window sticker says, "Actual results will vary for many reasons . . ." The real world, a virtually infinite combination of driving conditions and driver behavior, introduces a vast array of variables that influence the predicted numbers. The same goes for actual versus predicted 80/20 performance. This does not mean that you should reject Pareto's performance predictions; on the contrary, understand that the variations from 80/20 that you see in your reality-based quad charts reflect the influence of forces, decisions, actions, and other factors in the business, as well as in the market and the economy, that push and pull the data out of sync with "pure" 80/20 expectation.

The variations separating theory from fact are not errors but meaningful deltas that call for thoughtful analysis. Indeed, the differences between prediction and actuality should guide changes in strategy, tactics, policy, and personnel. The most direct messages the analysis provides relate to the sourcing, oversourcing, or desourcing of different customer and product quads based on levels of customer and product performance. To put it bluntly, allocate more sales resources to your A customers and fewer to your B customers.

Generations of common sense would urge you to identify your poorly performing quads, especially Quad 4, in which B customers buy B products, and allocate more resources to these in an attempt to revive and reinvigorate them. If this were a hospital, Quad 4 would contain your sickest patients and *would* merit generous resources. But Quad 4 is not a segment of a hospital, it is a segment of your business, one doing it more harm than good. Devote more resources to it, and you are increasing the harm by deepening the losses. It's worse than throwing good money after bad because the money you are throwing away is stolen from your best-performing quads. If you want to keep your current best customers and even add to their ranks, you had better start overserving their segment.

In the sample quad (figure 06-03), note that the performance of A customers buying A products in Quad 1 exceeds the Pareto prediction by about three percentage points. That's good! Right? But what does it mean for the business that just 248 customers (out of a total of 2,310) who buy just 2,692 products (out of a total of 31,419) are responsible for the high performance of Quad 1? At the same time, sales performance in Quads 2 and 3 is 3.1 and 2.9 percentage points (respectively) below the level the 80/20 Rule predicts. What product and resource allocation decisions should this motivate? Or look at Quad 4. It exceeds expectations by 2.8 percentage points. Perhaps more effort and resources should be devoted to moving some of these customers and products to a better quad. Perhaps demand justifies an increase in price. Or perhaps the overperformance of Quad 4 suggests that too many resources are being allocated to produce the "extra" 2.8 points.

You can do better. The measurements of activity in the four quads tell you where and how to improve. In chapter 7, we'll have much more to say about using the deltas between predicted and actual performance to guide strategic and tactical *actions*. For now, it is enough to understand and appreciate that Quad Charts offer you the Golden Rule.

The Golden Rule: Identify and Protect the Core Business While Eliminating Unnecessary Complexity

The 80/20 Rule is, for any business, the Golden Rule, and the Quad Chart is its graphical representation. Glance back at figure 06-03 and take a tour with me.

Quad 1 sits in the upper left of the chart. It consists of your A customers (the top 20% in terms of sales) and the A products they buy (again, the top 20%). This quad is often labeled "the Fort" because it generates roughly 80% of your revenue. What do you do with the Fort? You *hold it* as tightly as you can. You protect, defend, serve, and reinforce it above the other three quads. Your target should consist of devoting as close to 80% of your resources as you possibly can to serving Quad 1 so that it will *grow*. In our sample Quad Chart, the Fort in this real-world example accounts for 67.2% of sales, which amounts to some 200% of total profit.

Quad 2 occupies the upper right corner. It consists of your A customers and the B products they buy, which are SKUs that perform across the lower 80% of your business. This Quad is often called "the Necessary Evil." Representing just 12.9% of sales (in our real-world example), it may turn a modest profit or it may break even, so it does not stir much enthusiasm in the business.

Why, then, is it a *necessary* evil? In contrast to Quad 1, which is "simple," meaning that every product and every customer is a Class A performer, Quad 2 is "complex," producing a modest margin at best and break-even performance at worst. *That's* evil. But what makes it *necessary* is that A customers buy these products, and you don't want to drive *any* A customers away. So, you must stock this particular subset of B products.

Quad 3, at the lower left, is good for just 13.1% of sales but does turn over some 20% of total profit. These are the A products that B customers buy. If you want a label for this quad, you could do worse than call it "Okay, but Could Be Great." The trick is to keep this quad profitable by enforcing its simplicity. Make sales transactional; that means low touch, no consultative selling, maximizing online sales—whatever it takes to keep most of your human resources out of it.

Quad 4, in the lower right, houses your worst-performing customers and products—both strictly B-level. In our sample, 6.8% of sales are made here, which is 2.8 percentage points better than what 80/20 predicts. Strict 80/20 orthodoxy destines Quad 4 to vigorous simplification. This real-life example makes deciding on the degree of simplification more complicated. Thinking is required. As I suggested when I introduced figure 06-03, the overperformance of the quad might justify devoting some more resources to the quad to move the overperforming customers up to a better quad by generating more sales, pricing up some products rather than jettisoning them, or even that too many resources are being squandered on squeezing out a 2.8-point overperformance. The subtleties of simplification will be addressed in the next chapter.

SEATTLE, WE'VE GOT A PROBLEM

KING 5, the NBC-TV affiliate in Seattle, aired a story on October 28, 2024, that was subsequently posted on its website under the headline "Starbucks Pushes New Strategy As Sales Drop Across U.S." Sales had fallen 10% nationwide during fiscal Q4, a vertiginous slump in anyone's book. Brian Niccol, former Chipotle chairman and CEO, had been installed as Starbucks' new CEO, replacing Laxman Narasimhan, on September 9, 2024.

Niccol told KING 5 that he was launching a campaign he called "Back to Starbucks," which he described as an attempt to "welcome all our customers back and return to growth." Niccol believed that a "fundamental change" was called for, which amounted to reviving the original coffeehouse culture on which Starbucks had built its founding identity.

"People love Starbucks," Niccol told KING 5. "I've heard from some customers that we've drifted from our core, that we've made it harder to be a customer than it should be, and just not communicating with them."

Well, maybe. If going back to the core represents a true 80/20 simplification, it might just work. But KING 5 also talked directly to customers, including one who explained, "I don't go as often anymore because it's quite expensive." In fact, she "started to make more coffee at home." As a student just last year, she used to go "all the time." Now? "I bring instant coffee to my office . . . just kinda make it at my desk." She felt that she could not justify spending $7 or $8 for a cup of coffee.

Niccol himself acknowledged that the company had issues with worker pay (i.e., baristas asking for livable wages) and difficulty hiring adequate staff. He also wanted to improve the speed of customer service, reducing bottlenecks by improving "mobile order and pay," which, he believed, would make the visit to the coffeehouse more convenient and less stressful.

But most of all, Niccol reiterated the need to "remind people of why they love Starbucks."

Yup. But it may prove hard for people to remember that they love Starbucks when they are paying $8 for a cup of coffee served in a chain store (not a one-of-a-kind coffeehouse) by disgruntled staff who take their sweet time completing the transaction. Know what data you must measure. Your costs, your pricing, your competition's costs, their pricing, the disconnect between commodification (the chain store experience) and the authentic "hygge" of a genuine coffeehouse—all these factors should be measured. Armed with the data, you then apply these factors to the problem of reminding "people of why they love Starbucks."

This brings us to the complexity of leading a Values & Mission company. Mission-focused companies must be driven by a profit-focused vision, clearly defined by set revenue and profit targets. Value-focused companies prize the leader's values first and financial targets second. This rarely succeeds in a public company and virtually cannot succeed in a PE-sponsored company. Starbucks is a public company, which must therefore be focused on the bottom line. Yet the profitability of the company is linked to its relevant differentiator, which is based on a vision of value. Call it hygge, call it the *Cheers* effect ("a place where everybody knows your name"), call it anything but commodification. Anyone who steps up to lead Starbucks as its new Visionary must solve the problem of balancing values with financial goals, perfectly aligning the mission of the company with its vision.

The Visionary will know that he is succeeding when he no longer has a reason to keep reminding people that they love the company's product. That reason will disappear only when customers actually do love the product—again.

80/20: SOMETHING EVERYONE CAN LINE UP BEHIND

How often have you sought an explanation by asking for a picture? What does success *look* like? How does A stack up against B, C, D, and E? How do I get from Point A to Point E? Draw me a picture. Show me!

80/20 is a picture of success. 80/20 shows how A compares to B, C, D, and E. 80/20 shows you how to get from Point A to Point E. The 80/20 Quads present a snapshot of the business. You can see where everything *is*, and you can figure out where everything *should* be. Everyone in the organization—Visionary, Prophet(s), Operators, and those who report to each of them—can look at the same pictures. 80/20 both requires alignment and promotes alignment. It is an indispensable tool.

Chapter 7

ACTION

"Knowledge must come through action; you can have no test which is not fanciful, save by trial."

—Sophocles, *Trachiniae* (ca. 430 BC)

In chapter 6, we applied 80/20 to the data generated by your customers, products, sales, costs, profitability, markets, and regions for the purpose of "segmenting" your product/customer revenue into quads, which revealed the following:

In Quad 1, the performance of your A products bought by your A customers

In Quad 2, the performance of your B products bought by your A customers

In Quad 3, the performance of your A products bought by your B customers

In Quad 4, the performance of your B products bought by your B customers

Now, how do you use this segmentation to lead your enterprise to profitable growth? In other words, how do you convert data-based analytical insight into analysis-based action?

ACT WITH CONFIDENCE

At the risk of offering a blinding glimpse of the stunningly obvious, let me suggest that the best way to act with confidence is to know what to do.

Here's what to do: Serve Quad 1. This segment holds your highest-volume customers who buy your highest-volume products. This strategic intersection of A customers and A products is roughly 20% of your customer and product base, yet it is responsible for roughly 80% of your gross revenue. Address this disproportionate distribution by allocating to Quad 1 as near to 80% of your resources and effort as you can. That is, put the bulk of your investment into the segment that will yield the highest return.

This action is taken in accordance with the vision of the Visionary. It is an 80/20 vision, which, by definition, leads the enterprise in allocating its resources where they will produce the greatest growth. It is a data-based vision, implemented by the Prophet or Prophets, who show and instruct the Operators how to overserve the 80s by moving resources and effort up from less productive quads.

Designating and then overserving the top 20% of

customers and the products they buy is an act of the highest priority. Once this quad is properly overserved, the Prophet(s) and Operators must address the remaining three segments—Quads 2 through 4.

Bear in mind that Quad 1 is nicknamed "the Fort" because it must be held, protected, and strengthened. By definition, the Fort represents the core of the business, the place at which A customers buy A products.

Quad 2 is not to be spurned, however. Its nickname is the "Necessary Evil" because the B products in this quadrant are bought by A customers, the customer segment you want to keep happy. Still, acting in harmony with the Visionary's vision, the Prophet(s) and Operators understand that the company cannot afford to heap upon Quad 2 the kind and quantity of resources allocated to Quad 1. If the strategic move is to invest roughly 80% of your assets in serving the "critical" or "vital" 20% of customers and products that generate 80% of your revenue, you need to understand that 80% of your resources will no longer be available to the other three quads. Clearly, it cannot be part of the Visionary's plan to sacrifice 80% of customers and inventory to keep Quad 1 fat and happy. Compromise is called for.

There are two incentives to resource Quad 2 adequately. First, while the B products here are not in the top-performing 20% (if they were, they would be A products), they are still mostly on the upper end of the company's inventory. They may not generate the kind of revenue and margin Quad 1 creates, but they either turn a profit or break even. More important, their availability keeps a significant slice of the company's A customers happy and, therefore, loyal. An array of pricing and marketing tools and tactics are available to improve the sales and profitability of Quad 2. You may even be able to promote some of the B's to A's.

What, then, should you do with Quad 2? Figure out how to elevate it from a "Necessary Evil" to a decent source of growth that can promote some fraction of B products up to A level. Such promotion is an important aspect of growth, which Operators are especially well positioned to lead.

Quad 2 must be managed skillfully to provide the right level of resources to serve A customers and B products in this segment. In some companies, the performance of this quad rarely rises above break-even level. Since the principal strategic purpose here is to satisfy A customers, break-even must be considered acceptable performance. While the product may be a wash, it is not profit lost, but the happiness of high-volume customers earned. Under no circumstance, however, should the "Necessary Evil" be allowed to become "Pure Evil," which is what you must deem a quad that loses money.

Quad 3 stands Quad 2 on its head. It contains A products purchased by B customers. Where Quad 2 is a *Necessary* Evil, Quad 3 is a *Transactional* segment. Good business can be done here, provided it is transacted at low cost. Sales should be made with minimal (preferably zero) human interaction. Online transactions are most desirable here. The profit need not be strategic. Opportunistic money looks and smells just like strategic money. Do be aware, however, that profit is cannibalized in Quad 3 to the degree that sales lean toward time/money-consuming consultation and other human-mediated selling rather than brief, highly automated transactions.

Quad 4 is by definition the lowest-performing segment of the business. Even the best of Visionaries may be tempted to cut it loose, but this quad may benefit from more careful thought. It lends itself to creative marketing and pricing tactics capable of making some good money from the weakest segment of the business. For this reason, I label this quad with a nickname that is also an action decider: "Price Up or Out." Why *out*? It makes no sense to sell underperforming products to underperforming customers if no margin is possible.

VARIATIONS ON PRICE UP OR OUT

"Price Up or Out" is not the only tool in your Quad 4 toolbox. I like to use a set of tactics that, being an unapologetic Lee Marvin fan, I call "the Dirty Dozen." The first four focus on customers:

- *Can't Buy Me Love:* Ditch the insane business rule that you need to keep every customer you have, no matter what it costs you. Stop offering discounts to B customers, especially those B customers who buy unprofitable B products. Discounts narrow margin. Big discounts erase margin. If you are losing money on each sale, what *are* you thinking of? Both Quads 3 and 4 call for pricing up or tossing out. Discounting is not a strategic answer.

- *Money for Nothing:* Always minimize the cost of selling to B customers. This tactic declines to pay sales commissions on most B-customer trades.
- *Money (That's What I Want):* When margins are tight, simplify sales and fulfilment. For Quads 3 and 4, you might require up-front payment by credit card—and, if the spirit moves you, tack on a fee as well.
- *All the Small Things:* Sometimes you can squeeze value out of a low-margin sale by setting a minimum-order quantity on some B merchandise. Engineer sales terms that make selling these dogs worth your while.

The next eight Dirty Dozen moves focus on products:

- *Circle of Life:* Substitute A products from a preferred vendor for equivalent B products wherever possible. This pushes customers to buy from your A-product segments.

- *No Scrubs:* This is heavy artillery. You can't call it a tool because it is a weapon. Just drop B products sold to B customers that have no strategic value. Throwing good money after bad is a loser.
- *Ain't No Mountain High Enough:* Exercise a combination of caution and chutzpah with this one. Before jettisoning a failing B product, try not merely pricing it up, but way, *way* up. Any customer can have this item, provided they are willing to pay the price.
- *Take It or Leave It:* This tactic calls for a bit of imagination. Don't dump a feeble piece of B merchandise, and don't price it up either. Instead, offer it in a single standard package size. Never break this bulk. If customers want it, they must take it on your terms.
- *Time After Time:* Another inventive tactic is to stop the piecemeal, on-demand filling of orders on deep-B goods. Instead, aggregate them, withholding fulfilment until you have enough orders in hand to build a margin. Sure, the customer can purchase this product, provided she is patient.

- *Don't You (Forget About Me):* Restrict sales of weak items to scheduled days. Don't scramble for unprofitable business.
- *My Way:* Limit availability of certain B products to very, very few standard option packages. No mix-and-match options. Reducing complexity reduces your inventory overhead. Sell the item *your* way or not at all.
- *You've Got Another Thing Coming:* Niche or specialized B products can sometimes be made profitable by packaging them in sets. Want that weird screwdriver that fits just one tool? It comes packaged with all these other screwdrivers. Offer the set. Customers can always throw away what they don't want.

GROW THROUGH SIMPLIFICATION

Growth is not about getting bigger. It's about getting simpler. That means focusing first on the 20% of customers and products that generate roughly 80% of your revenue and then strategically allocating the rest of your available resources to the 80% of customers and products that generate a still-significant fraction of your revenue.

Desperate companies often try to cut their way to a turnaround. When margins evaporate, the picture of severed heads rolling has considerable appeal. But I'm here to tell you that you cannot cut your way to growth—at least not with a chainsaw. You need a scalpel to carry out a survivable, beneficial surgery. Any successful surgery is a strategic operation. It cuts out only what is unhealthy, a drag on the survival of the patient. In a business looking for turnaround growth, your incisions must be meticulously strategic. The quads will identify the customers and products that are generating revenue. They will also identify those that can be de-resourced and/or priced up (or treated with an appropriate application from the Dirty Dozen toolbox).

The quads will also reveal the segment of customers/products that should be cut away. Obviously, serving any customer incurs costs. Growth results when only productive customers—customers who produce more revenue than cost—are served. Most of us in business have a natural inclination to create customers and then keep them—at any cost. The promptings of nature are not always benevolent, however. When keeping a customer fails to pay for itself, keeping that customer begins to kill the company. Strictly applying 80/20 will keep your business focused on strategic reality.

Don't be afraid to drop unprofitable products, or to lose unprofitable customers who buy only unprofitable products. Don't hesitate to treat B customers differently from

A customers. All customers must be treated fairly, but all customers should also be treated strategically, and fair treatment is not always equal treatment. This means that A customers buying A products, the 20% of customers who produce 80% of your revenue, should be strategically overserved. This is fair treatment, but not equal, and necessitates strategically de-resourcing B customers by reallocating sales and service resources from the lower quads to Quad 1 and making B-level sales low-touch, requiring less human involvement (and automating transactions wherever possible). Study the Dirty Dozen and design selling terms that favor the business by pricing up low-volume products until they realize a margin. If you cannot make money on a product, drop it. If some B customers leave you, bid them farewell and Godspeed.

None of this is about rewarding "good" and punishing "bad" customers. It is about growing the business. Thus, Quad 4 sales (B products to B customers) must be made with minimum resource commitment from the sales force or customer service. This is also true, though less extreme, for Quad 3, A products purchased by B customers; however, A customers purchasing B products in Quad 2 are entitled to some degree of sales force commitment and other support.

So, thinking is required. Is it possible to oversimplify your business? Absolutely, and this is a danger to be carefully guarded against. The sweet spot at which you are aiming is a strategy that devotes 80% of the company's resources to the

20% of customers who produce 80% of your gross revenue. But why not just devote 100% of your assets to Quad 1 and kick out the lower 80% of customers altogether?

Never let the best become the enemy of the good. Quad 1 is the best: your best customers buying your best products. You can safely assume that Quad 1 is simple and cannot be simplified further. Every customer and product in this quad is productive.

Quad 2 is less simple because it is not an AA segment but an AB segment, in which A customers are buying B products—by the numbers, not as profitable as A products. Nevertheless, some of these B products still produce profit, and you have the added incentive that some of your best customers demand these products. The complexity isn't ideal, but it not only leaves room for profit, it also represents an investment in making some of your best customers happy and more inclined to be loyal.

Quad 1 is simple. Quad 2 has room for some simplification. Quads 3 and 4 offer more opportunity for simplification because they create unnecessary complexity that bleeds resources away from the A products and customers. Quad 3 is a prime candidate for the Dirty Dozen. Quad 4 may be served by these tactics as well but is also ripe for pricing up or dropping altogether. Strategic reductions are far less about jettisoning products or laying off employees than they are about reallocating resources. Employees liberated from Quads 3 and 4 are available to overresource Quads 1 and 2.

BABIES AND BATHWATER

Everybody knows at least one thing about babies and bathwater: Don't discard the former with the latter. Many folks who should know better, however, take a simplistic view of simplification, assuming that if some simplification is good, more is even and invariably better:

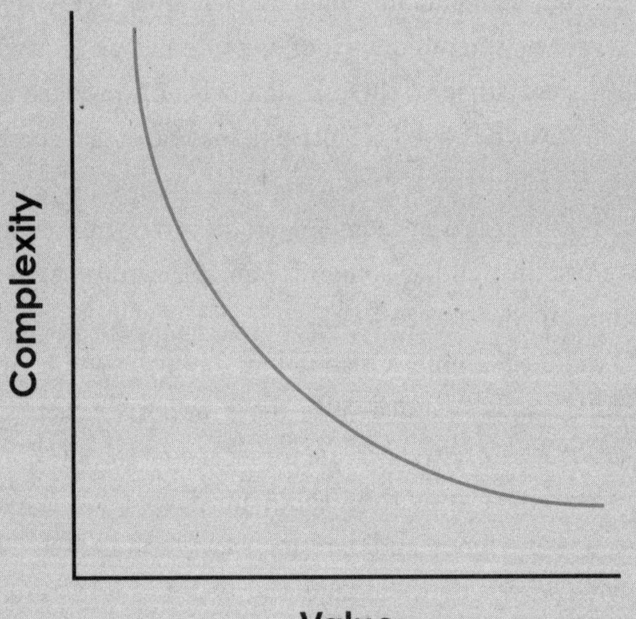

Figure 07-01

A false visualization of complexity.

Reality is more complex. There's a peak (technically called "the mode") at which the balance between complexity and simplicity yields maximum value:

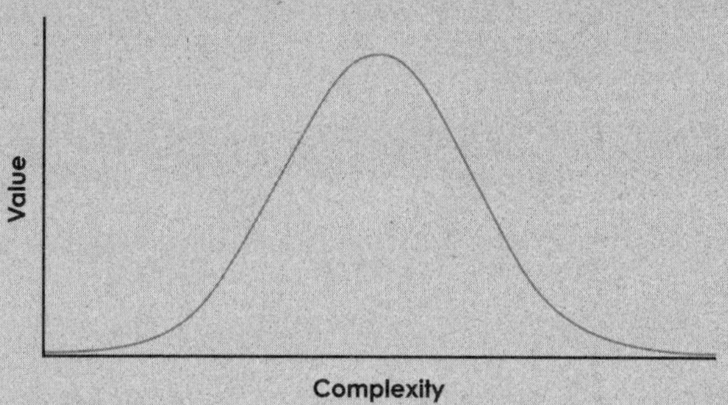

Figure 07-02

A true visualization of complexity.

Applying 80/20 can minimize the downward side of the curve, ensuring that the business is investing in the 20% of products and customers that produce 80% of revenue. Anyone who has looked at a treasure map knows that "X marks the spot." In the case of optimizing the business for strategic growth, X marks the point where at complexity (for instance, variety of products, models, and variations offered) creates the greatest value. Adding complexity beyond this point reduces value. You should strategically de-resource your investment in products and customers who occupy the space to the right of the X.

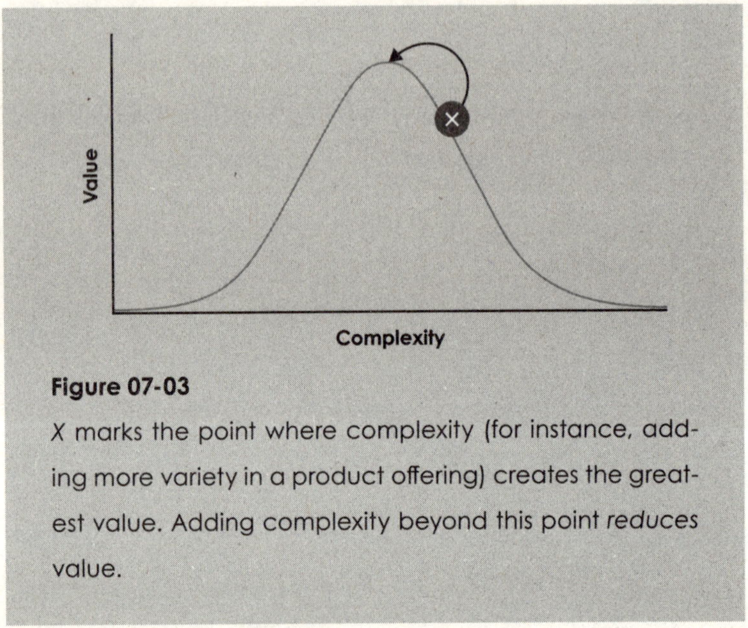

Figure 07-03

X marks the point where complexity (for instance, adding more variety in a product offering) creates the greatest value. Adding complexity beyond this point *reduces* value.

STEP 1: TAKE AIM

The overall goal is self-evident: Make money rather than lose money. That is what the whole PGOS process is about. Step 1 in the process, before 80/20 is even applied, is setting a financial goal for the next three to five years. For the purposes of planning, the value of the goal is obvious: It is a target. This means that there is a measurable distance between where the company is right now and where it is supposed to be in three to five years. The space between the present state and the future goal is a gap. Knowing where you are, where you want to be, and the measurable distance between the two means that you need never be lost. So, gather the financial data required to determine the present state of your company: *where you are.* Compile the data relating to current revenue, current margin, and current EBITDA (earnings before interest, taxes, depreciation, and amortization), and compare this data to the future, as projected in future revenue, margin, and EBITDA.

Present, future, and the gap in between. That gap is not a mere void; it is the measure of where you need to be within the time frame the Visionary has set. In the first 100 days of launching your growth strategy, you must analyze the gap. This requires you to do the following:

1. Identify the objectives that you need to achieve to reach your future-state financial goal.
2. Analyze, for each of the future-state objectives you identify, the present state of these objectives. What is being done currently in each of these areas?
3. Figure out what you need to do differently from what you are doing today to successfully bridge the gap between the present state and the desired future state (i.e., your goal).

Practically everyone I know in business talks about how sick and tired they are of hearing the expression "move the needle." And yet, these very same people—myself included—keep thinking in terms of this metaphor. It is, after all, a meaningful concept. Once you have data on where you are and where you want to be—by the numbers—you must determine what actions will *move the needle* up from the present-state numbers to the desired future-state numbers. Break down the distance between present and future into steps, quarter by quarter and year by year. Application of 80/20 analysis is your most effective tool for completing the steps to bridge the gap (figure 07-04).

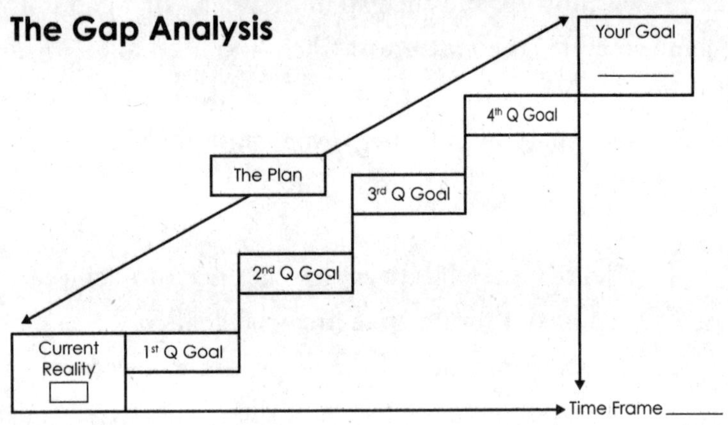

Figure 07-04

The Gap Analysis.

THINKING IS REQUIRED (BUT DON'T OVERTHINK THIS)

Data is the essential basis for all strategically valid actions. Strategy cannot exist without adequately interpreted data. But I advise you, in setting your goal, not to sweat the numbers beyond a rapid 80/20 analysis and a quick gap analysis. The most important thing about any goal is that it is a goal—a target, an aspiration, a marker of a future the organization needs to share that is better than the present.

What about the numbers?

Well, they need to be at least plausible. They don't need to be exactly right, which is a good thing, because they are about the future and, by definition, aspirational rather than factual. The goal is a bull's-eye target, but you don't need to measure that bull's-eye's diameter in millimeters. Make it reasonable. Your idea of reasonable may seem to some too big, too small, or just right. All you really need is something to aim at. As time goes by and you and your business close the gap, you can refine the goal. As you draw closer to it, the target will become clearer. You do not have all the answers, but you do have a process that will lead the organization in gathering the data, applying valid analytical procedures to the data, transforming analysis into action, and correcting course on the fly. So keep measuring the gap. Apply 80/20 to measure the profitability of your customers and the products they buy, and make adjustments accordingly. Do this, and you will create improvement.

And that goal?

It's only money. Come up with an amount. Achieving the goal requires careful analysis, tough decisions, courageous commitment, hard work, and hard thinking. But setting the goal is just a matter of sizing the prize by answering two financial questions:

1. Where are you now?
2. Where do you want to be in three to five years?

What's so magical about three to five years? Nothing at all. Some firms like to work on three-year business plans, others prefer five. I'm sure you can find companies that choose other time frames. Choose one and size the prize accordingly.

Sometimes, even if you are the Visionary, the author of the sacred script, you will be handed the goal. Take me, for instance. Revisiting Rolling Thunder, the suite of companies for which private equity hired me as CEO, I was given a leadership assignment to produce within five years a 3× multiple on invested cash (MOIC). Expressing this multiple as a financial goal was a simple matter of calculating the EBITDA required to hit that 3× MOIC within five years. It took a matter of minutes to make the calculation: Rolling Thunder would have to generate $2.3 billion in revenue with 19% margins and some $450 million in EBITDA by year five. (We simply determined our current EBITDA and then multiplied the result by three to get our goal.)

While five years seems like ample time to reach our 3× MOIC, we had to first position the company for a turnaround that would get us there. This positioning needed to be completed in a hundred days, roughly a single quarter. As mentioned in the paragraph above, the math was quick and simple. But we needed to have some idea as to the feasibility of the turnaround. Data from the latest annual report was a sufficient basis to determine the feasibility. Later, we would need to achieve a fuller situation assessment, but, for now, under the gun of a hundred-day timetable, we had a goal and could use it to *frame* a strategy.

STEP 2: FRAME A STRATEGY

Once we had a goal, we knew Step 1 had been completed. We had to generate $2.3 billion in revenue with 19% margins and $450 million in EBITDA by year five. The purpose of Step 2 would be to rough-frame a strategy that would get us there.

We had a proven guide: 80/20. The core of the strategy was therefore straightforward. Simplify the business so that we could focus not on the trivial many (the 80% of causes that produced just 20% of productive results) but on the critical few (the 20% of causes that produced 80% of productive results).

I am not here to write the history of Rolling Thunder, but to provide an example of what it means to set a goal for a business. Whatever else a business goal is, it is a number. For Rolling Thunder, getting to this number was a simple calculation using a financial spec created by a private equity owner. Every specific situation is unique, however. Different factors, purposes, values, motives, and aspirations may have a bearing on the goal. No matter. In the end, it must be centered on a number. Rolling Thunder gives us that number quickly, so that we can move past the debates that often swirl about a goal, and proceed directly to the strategy that, as framed by the CEO/Visionary and based on historic and current data and the analysis of same, was to simplify the business as calculated according to the 80/20 principle. What follows, then, is not restricted to the example of Rolling Thunder or any other particular business. It is a template that can be applied generally.

The Prophets must own the process, tools, and techniques; they must train everyone in their use. Think of the Prophets as high school shop teachers, who show the class how to run the tools without losing limbs or digits. They train the trainers.

For all that they do, the Visionary and the Prophets do not *build* the strategy. That will be led by the company's Operators (all members of the upper-management cadre), who in turn convey the Visionary's vision by instructing and inspiring their teams, who are most immediately responsible for executing the vision and producing the results.

At this step, framing the strategy, the Visionary and their team have already assessed the current state of the business to determine what is and is not working so that resources can be moved to *what is*. Using 80/20 converts this descriptive language—*what is and is not working*—to a quantified division: the 80% of resources, products, and customers that have a trivial positive impact on profitable growth, versus the 20% of these people and things having a critical positive impact. Based on this division, the company's Operators (again, typically COOs or division heads) would lead the formulation of a simplification strategy that allows the business to allocate as close to 80% of its resources to serving the 20% of customers and products that produce 80% of its revenue. This deliverable is the framework of a strategy to position the company to earn the right to grow. The Prophet (or Prophets) will train each Operator in how to create the strategy and disseminate it to the Operator's team, which runs the everyday business. Overseen by the Prophet(s), the Operators must train, mentor, and direct their reports to successfully deploy the company strategy.

STEP 3: MAKE TOMORROW DIFFERENT FROM TODAY

You have created—or roughed out at any rate—a strategy whose purpose is to make tomorrow different from today. The trigger for a new strategy is an awareness that "today" is not good enough. It is not where you aspire—or maybe urgently need—to be.

This brings you to Step 3: creating the structure that more fully articulates and enables a vision of tomorrow, the desired or desperately needed future state of the business. The vision is developed from the strategic objectives articulated in Step 2 and uses them to lay out the initiatives required to achieve them. Step 3 must deliver an executable strategy to realize the vision and mission of the business by implementing the correct initiatives to achieve the correct objectives. The ongoing test of whether these components of the vision and mission are being achieved is the extent to which the business moves toward the financial goal set in Step 1. This movement is the key metric in assessing the success of the strategy.

The strategy laid out in Step 2 addressed strategic alignment—the focus of the company on delivering profitable organic growth, and the execution of that focus. This is the *what* of the strategy. Step 3 addresses *how* organic growth will achieve profitable share gain in the market by lowering operating costs and growing sales organically. Step 3 may also go on to outline a plan for investing in further growth beyond what is organically available to the company. Geographic (territory) expansion, product line expansion, or both typically entail making the strategic case for mergers and acquisitions.

STRATEGIC DELIVERABLES

Think of your new strategy as a suitcase of deliverables. They address *where* the business will compete, *what* capabilities are required to make it competitive, and *why* the business will win. If all of the following are neatly tucked into this suitcase, the strategy is ready for action:

- Mission and vision
- Prior-year strategy overview
- Business environment assessment
- Strategic priorities summary, including strategic objectives, definition/scoping and rationale, value potentially at risk/potential value to be created
- Strategic priorities, consisting of two to five (three is a good target) strategic initiatives, likely including initiatives for strengthening the core of the business, improving market attractiveness, and improving competitive position
- Key programs/projects, actions, resources, organizational implications, and investments required to execute on the strategic priorities and initiatives
- Three- to five-year strategic financial forecast
- Draft of strategic initiative Gantt charts, including hypothesis, high-level timing, and resource requirements
- Market expansion opportunities (M&A), with risks summarized
- A concluding bullet list of critical success factors

MOVE FROM DIVERGENT TO CONVERGENT

80/20 is a thing of beauty. It reveals how to focus the business on Quad 1—the Fort—while allocating remaining resources to Quads 2 and 3 and approaching Quad 4 strategically to make the very best of it. Nevertheless, 80/20 has its limitations. Apportioning resources for optimum productivity still requires thought. 80/20 is a good guide but an incompetent dictator. Thinking is required.

In fact, two kinds of thinking are required: divergent and convergent. Brainstorming is the most familiar form of divergent thinking: putting key people together in a room and asking them to generate as many ideas as possible, candidly and uncensored. The goal is to surface all the possibilities and inventory the strategic options available to the business.

When the brainstorm dies down, shift from divergent to convergent thinking. Review the ideas generated in the divergent phase. Discard what will *not* work as well as what is *not* imperative. Winnow the options to just two or three proposed strategic initiatives for the first full year of a strategic plan. If the thinking group demands it, retain as many as five objectives.

Take your short list of surviving initiatives and work them up into statements of strategic objectives and initiatives. These statements are the first key deliverables of the convergent thinking process. They should be reasonably complete statements of *what*, *when*, *why*, *who*, and *where*.

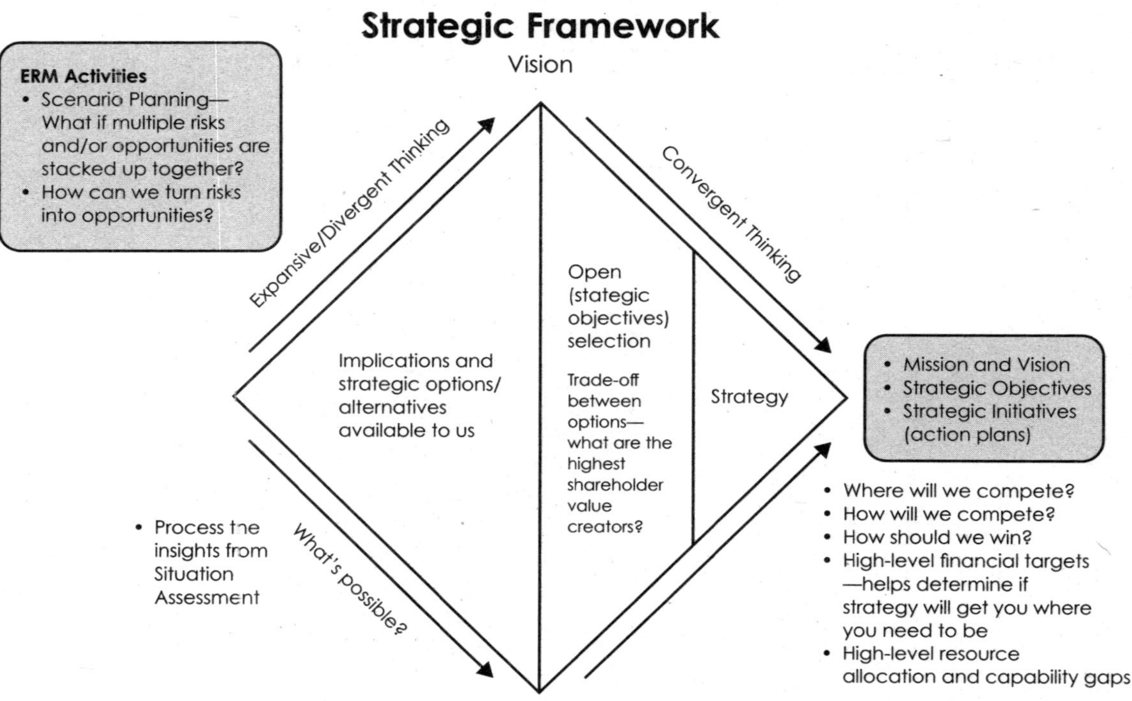

Figure 07-05

Divergent/Convergent thinking cycle.

THREE KEY QUESTIONS TO ANSWER NOW

The convergent-thinking phase following the divergent phase is key to defining initiatives for the first full year of the strategic plan, which must answer three questions:

1. Where will we compete?
2. How will we compete?
3. Why will we win?

How do you know your answers are correct? You will not know until you have applied the strategic initiatives formulated in the divergent–convergent step. The first hundred days of your new strategic plan should at least begin to validate or invalidate the initiatives. If all goes well, you should see progress but not perfection. Monitor, modify, and tweak.

Chapter 8

RESULTS

"It is only by risking our persons from one hour to another that we live at all. And often enough our faith beforehand in an uncertified result is the only thing that makes the result come true."

—William James,
The Principles of Psychology (1890)

In a February 1952 Gallup poll, President Harry S. Truman earned a job approval of 22%, the lowest that polling organization had (and has) ever recorded. The public's estimation of him as a decision maker was encapsulated in 1948 by what today would be dubbed an attack meme: "To err is Truman." Yet, in a 2021 C-SPAN survey of American presidents, HST was ranked as the sixth-best chief executive in American history, behind Lincoln, Washington, Franklin Roosevelt, Theodore Roosevelt, and Eisenhower, putting him above the likes of Thomas Jefferson, John F. Kennedy, Ronald Reagan, and Barack Obama. In anybody's book, this makes Truman a great president.

Little wonder. For HST's presidential decisions included some of the most consequential in history, beginning with the decision to use atomic weapons to end World War II, continuing through his bold action to racially integrate the US Armed Forces, thereby inaugurating the Civil Rights movement, and his implementation of the massive Marshall Plan, which not only rescued a war-ravaged Europe but saved it from Soviet conquest and confirmed the 20th century as the "American Century." In an essay that, on his instructions, remained unpublished until after his death, Truman described his decision-making process:

> First of all, the president has got to get all the information he can possibly get as to what's best for the most people in the country, and that takes both basic character and self-education. He's not only got to decide what's right according to the principles by which he's been raised and educated, but he also has to be willing to listen to a lot of people, all kinds of people, and find out what effect the decision he's about to make will have on the people. And when he makes up his mind that his decision is correct, he mustn't let himself be moved from that decision under any consideration. He must go through with that

> program and not be swayed by the pressures that are put on him by people who tell him that his decision is wrong. If the decision is wrong, all he has to do is get some more information and make another decision, because he's got to have the ability to change his mind and start over. That's the only way in the world a man can carry on as chief executive.

Any Rule of 3 Visionary should commit this paragraph to memory, because it's all here. You begin by getting the data: all the relevant information. You bring to it your experience, your intellect, and your moral compass. Then you seek opinions from a diverse range of people you respect. You listen carefully to those who will be most affected by your decision.

That's it.

Now you make your decision and, having decided, follow through to implement it, steadfastly refusing to be swayed.

Note the very end of Truman's paragraph: Make the decision, implement the decision, and don't be swayed. Recognize, however, that the decision may be wrong. If it is, go out and get more information. *Then make another decision.*

Truman argued that the president, the CEO, or any final decision maker must be prepared and willing to make a new and different decision based on the results of the original decision. Any good decision is the product of the real world; however, only after the actions created by the decision are released into the wild of that real world can you discover how effective, ineffective, productive, or destructive that decision was. The Visionary cannot give up being the Visionary—it's now their role. But the Visionary can, if need be, start over with a new decision. Now, as Truman and all effective Visionaries understand, that new decision may carry over whatever was good about the original decision. It may simply be an amended version of that decision. Or it may be substantially or even entirely new. Either way, the new decision must be based on data, the reality created by the original decision versus the new reality you want or need to create.

An enterprise advances only through decision making. A business *may* fail if the decisions are bad, but it *will* fail if no decisions are made or if they are acted upon indecisively. Bad decisions can be corrected with good (or at least better) decisions. Realistically, we can strive for perfection, but we must accept progress as a win. So, the leaders of the enterprise must be simultaneously decisive and willing to change their minds based on results.

The courage, will, and energy to change your mind is essential to evaluating decisions and deciding whether (and how) to make new decisions. The best way to evaluate the effect of your decisions is to create a periodic feedback loop that runs backward from the business plan to the situation assessment. With a situation assessment freshly informed by new information, the Visionary is positioned to create a modified or, sometimes, entirely new strategic framework and to align the Prophet(s) and Operators executing it.

BETWEEN A BAD DECISION AND NO DECISION, CHOOSE THE BAD DECISION

No enterprise advances without decision making. Bad decisions *may* wound a business, possibly even fatally. However, the absence of decisions *will* certainly kill a business dead. A bad decision can be changed. No decision is a zero, nothing, and nothing will come of nothing.

A decision that proves to be bad still has value. At the very least, it tells you what to *stop* doing, and usually at least hints at *what* to do. The Visionary (like Prophets and Operators) needs the data produced by unproductive or damaging results to evaluate prospective new decisions and choose the best from among them. The periodic feedback loop running backward from the business plan to the situation assessment uses the new information produced by the original decision's failure to guide modification or replacement of the current business plan.

PLAN, DO, CHECK, ACT

The periodic feedback loop that PDCA—Plan, Do, Check, Act—prescribes is not new. It was developed back in the 1930s by Walter Shewhart, a physicist, engineer, and statistician. In him, these three fields were mutually reinforcing. Indeed, while his training in engineering and physics was academic, he was self-taught in statistics (as were most statisticians of that era), and thus his approach to statistics was grounded in the laws of nature (physics) and their practical application (engineering). He applied his intensively real-world statistical approach to industrial quality control and developed PDCA, which took everything he knew about statistics and put it into four sequential actions: Plan, Do, Check, Act.

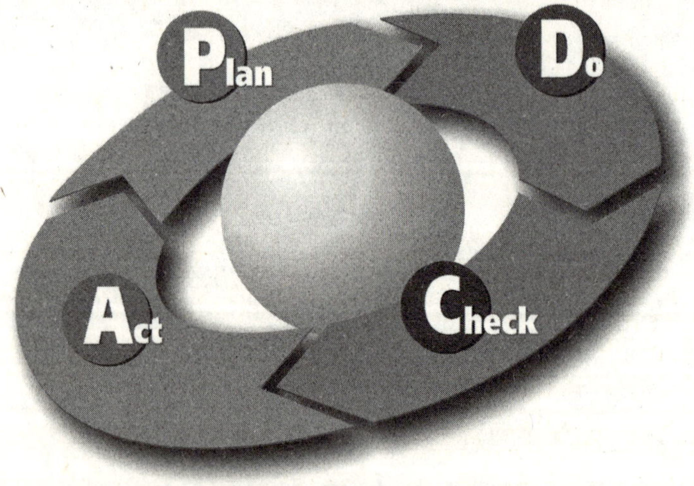

Figure 08-01

The PDCA cycle.

Strangely enough, PDCA did not break out of the industrial silo until the 1950s, when it was picked up by another engineer/statistician turned management guru, W. Edwards Deming, who applied PDCA to the entire field of management. What had been called the Shewhart Cycle became the Deming Wheel.

Loaded with data in the form of KPIs (Key Performance Indicators), PDCA gives your organization a productive cadence capable of driving continuous improvement. KPIs are different for different industries and businesses. Common examples, however, include:

- **Conversion rate:** the rate at which customer contact is converted into sales. This is a major KPI for digital businesses with commerce websites, for instance.
- **Customer satisfaction (CSAT):** measures the quality of service of a segment, a team, or an entire business
- **Customer retention rate:** measures how often customers return to a business to make a purchase
- **Net promoter score (NPS):** measures what percentage of customers would recommend a product to others—a measurement of customer referral
- **Average handle time:** measures the time for a call center agent to answer a customer support call, address it, and disconnect
- **Average resolution time:** measures how long it takes for a live chat operator to resolve a customer issue

- **Revenue growth:** growth, plus or minus, over a given period, such as quarter-over-quarter
- **Revenue per client:** a useful metric for 80/20 analysis to establish performance expectations
- **Profit margin:** among the most basic of KPIs

As mentioned, the KPIs you choose to measure depend on the nature of your business, but an essential rule of thumb will make your choice more meaningful. Each KPI should achieve five SMART objectives. The KPI should be *Specific, Measurable, Assignable, Realistic,* and *Time Related.* If a proposed KPI does not meet all five objectives, it should be revised until it does, and if it cannot be revised to this point, it should be discarded. So, interrogate each KPI under consideration:

- **Is its objective *specific*?** Why is the goal important? Who must be involved in achieving it? What additional resources will be required?
- **Is the objective *measurable*?** As noted earlier, Peter Drucker, a Deming disciple, reportedly said (or quoted V. F. Ridgway), "What gets measured gets managed." This is because only the measurable can be meaningfully assessed and acted upon.
- **Is the objective *assignable*?** Each KPI must have specific action items and action steps assigned to it, which, in turn, must be delegated to accountable managers (and others) capable of executing them. If

the business lacks personnel with the needed competencies and capacity for the objective, either the objective must be discarded or appropriate personnel must be trained or acquired.

- **Is the objective *realistic*?** "A man's reach should exceed his grasp," the poet Robert Browning wrote, and this quotation has often been used to encourage reach-for-the-stars aspiration. Achieving difficult objectives may be worthwhile, but impossible or unfeasible objectives are not SMART. No KPI would intentionally set people up for failure.
- **Is the objective *time related*?** Not only must a KPI be measurable, it must be measurable in terms of time. Each objective requires a timeline terminating in a deadline. Without this, it is not possible to effectively coordinate multiple tasks.

With meaningful KPIs in place, you are ready to work the segments of PDCA.

PLAN

Understand the problem or opportunity. As a prelude to planning, advance understanding through these five steps:

1. **Establish a strategic link.** Determine how acting on the problem or opportunity will contribute to achieving the business strategy and business plan.

2. **Comprehend the current state.** Understand all dimensions of the problem or opportunity in question. This constitutes an assessment of the issue.
3. **Project the desired future state.** Having established the current state of the problem or opportunity, envision the desired future state. Clearly define the desired change by setting goals or targets that must be achieved to realize whatever business value you must gain.
4. **Identify the right team.** Put together a team capable of providing multiple perspectives and expertise on the problem or opportunity.
5. **Secure leadership support.** Garner alignment among all leadership (Visionary to Prophet to Operators) to invest the needed personnel, time, and other resources to solve the problem or realize the opportunity.

After completing these five steps, you are prepared to definitively identify root causes of the problem or principal drivers of the opportunity. Begin with divergent thinking and inventory as many potential causes/drivers as possible. Seek feedback and multiple viewpoints from people both inside and outside of the team. Collect and study relevant data to determine which of the causes/drivers are worth pursuing. Switch to convergent thinking to compile this short list. For addressing problems, use your short list of causes to identify appropriate countermeasures. This requires shifting back to divergent thinking to develop an expansive list of possible actions to address root causes. Next, shift back to convergent thinking to prioritize the items on your list. Filter the list by criteria essential to achieving the future state you have defined as well as by resource limitations.

Now you are poised to build an action plan. Rough out a 30,000-foot overview sufficient to give you an understanding of actions required to advance the business toward your set goal. Break down the high-level elements into multiple tasks or steps; these are the granular bricks of the plan. For each brick, ensure alignment with all stakeholders. Depending on the scope of the problem or opportunity, achieving perfect alignment may require starting with the Rule of 3 principals—Visionary, Prophet(s), and Operators. More likely, however, the alignment can and should begin lower, by aligning a Prophet with one or more Operators.

DO

Pull the trigger.

Do: Execute the plan. If dealing with a problem, implement the countermeasures. If leveraging an opportunity, take the action on which the Rule of 3 principals have aligned. In either case, scrupulously monitor the results.

Check: Evaluate the results of implementing the countermeasures or activating the plan. You are looking to verify or refute the hypothesis and predictions that drove the plan. Evaluate the benefits, the liabilities, and the timeliness of realizing them. Learn all you can from the results to improve the team's problem-solving capabilities. What worked? What failed? And, either way, why?

Act: Determine the next steps in executing the business strategy or plan through continuous improvement. Based on the results—the degree or lack of improvement—push ahead with or amend your plan. Never stop collecting data.

BELIEVE IN MIRACLES

The purpose of the PDCA feedback loop is to answer a blatantly obvious question: "Are we achieving our plan?" Japan's defeat in World War II was devastating, but its economic recovery in the years between their surrender and the end of the Cold War that followed it was so sweeping that the world called it the Japanese Miracle.

This is one miracle in which you can believe, for the simple reason that it was driven by remarkable management systems. Such systems were exemplified most influentially by the systems at Toyota Industries, practices that measured performance with remarkable accuracy and speed, so that the measurements could be readily converted into analysis that drove specific actions.

From the late 1960s into the 1970s, Toyota founder/CEO

Sakichi Toyoda, an exemplary Visionary, introduced and deployed what he called the Five Whys. As 80/20 applies the ratio of the critical versus the trivial to cut through mere assumptions, gut feelings, and received wisdom to measurably improve performance and create measurable growth, the Five Whys cut through superficial appearances to get to the root cause of problems and issues that interfere with the successful implementation of a business plan. The approach holds that most failures can be reversed and problems solved by asking *why* five times.

For instance, there is a water puddle on the shop floor.

Why?

As it turns out, the obvious answer (just look up) is that **an overhead pipe is leaking.**

But we still have four more *whys* to go. So, the question is asked a second time: *Why?* This repetition does not reject the first answer but invites a deeper explanation that digs in the direction of a root cause: **The water pressure in the pipe is too high.**

But *Why?*

This third question prompts close examination, which yields the discovery that **the control valve is faulty.**

Okay. *Why?*

Now we need an answer for what caused the control valve to fail. **Our control valves have not been tested.**

Reasonable response, but not yet at root level. A fifth *Why?* uncovers the reason for the failure to test the control valves: **The control valves have not been listed on the maintenance schedule.**

The discovery of this, the root cause of a puddle on the shop floor, contains (as is true of most causes) its own solution, namely to **put a control valve inspection on the maintenance schedule**. When? Well, there's a puddle on the floor, so ***Do it now.***

The Five Whys cut through the trivial to arrive at the critical. A related step-by-step problem-solving procedure from the "Toyota Way" was dubbed the "A3 Process." Its namesake is a sheet of paper trimmed to A3 size (close to 11" × 17"), which Toyota managers had long used to scribble ideas, plans, and goals.

The first step of the A3 Process is to identify the problem or need. The second is to determine the current state of the situation by observing and documenting the work processes involved. When the documentation is complete, the relevant team gathers around a whiteboard to lay out each production process step.

Having identified the problem and the work processes associated with it, the next task is to quantify the magnitude of the issue. For instance, we discover that "*X* deliveries to customers are late." The data over time should be presented graphically to create a literal quantified picture of the current state of the situation. Using this, the team can start digging to the root cause. The following questions can help reveal the pain points:

- What information do we need to work more effectively?
- Where are the delays in the work process?

- Where are the delays longest?
- Where are we failing to communicate adequately?

Once the pain points are exposed, apply the Five Whys to dig down to the root causes. With these revealed, take action:

1. **Formulate countermeasures (make changes in your processes) to root out root causes.** Change processes to move the organization closer to optimum by addressing root causes directly. You must plan these changes meticulously and specify the intended outcome. Once it is specified, lay out a plan for achieving it. Review the connections and coordination among all personnel responsible for steps in the process, beginning with the Prophet(s) and Operators. Clarify, simplify, or otherwise remedy inefficiencies and other causes of delay throughout the process.
2. **Define your target state.** Having formulated the necessary changes in the process, define your target state with a process map, which notes precisely where the changes in the process are occurring so they can be observed and evaluated in real time.
3. **Draw up a revised deployment plan**, including a task list to put the process changes in place, a roster of who is responsible for what, and due dates for the completion of each task.
4. **Create a follow-up plan, which specifies all**

predicted outcomes. This step allows the teams to verify improvement. If there is no improvement, the teams must review whether the implementation plan was executed, the target condition was realized, and the expected results were achieved.

5. **After completing the A3 Process, the results must be reported to all teams involved in executing the improvement plan.** Prophet(s) and operators must be aligned, and operators must ensure alignment of their teams. Consensus on the new or modified processes must be built and verified.

After full buy-in is secured, the new process is ready to be implemented. This is not the final step in the improvement journey, however. The results of implementation must be evaluated. If they vary substantially from expectations, ask the Five Whys to discover why. Perform the necessary research to answer each of the whys. Use this feedback to change your processes until those modified processes enable the team, division, or company to achieve whatever strategic goals have been set.

TAP THE GENIUS OF EINSTEIN

The Five Whys and A3 can solve many problems or make accessible many opportunities a Visionary, Prophet, or Operator may encounter. But you need to call on no less a figure than Albert Einstein to raise your PDCA game to the next level.

Albert Einstein was a theoretical physicist, meaning that he typically dealt in hypotheticals. He decided he needed to bring the imaginary universe of the hypothetical down to earth, to the bread-and-butter realm of data-based science. To do this he adopted the *Gedankenexperiment* technique—literally the "thought experiment"—for planning in the context of "What if?" or the future. Although the thought experiment is an exercise of the imagination, it is controlled by the rules of real-world logic. That is, cause and effect still apply.

Figure 08-02

Albert Einstein, genius.

So, how do you apply the thought experiment to your business?

The Pareto Principle tells us that there's a very high likelihood that just ~20% of your customers and the products they buy are responsible for ~80% of your revenue, as the two pyramids in figure 08-03 illustrate.

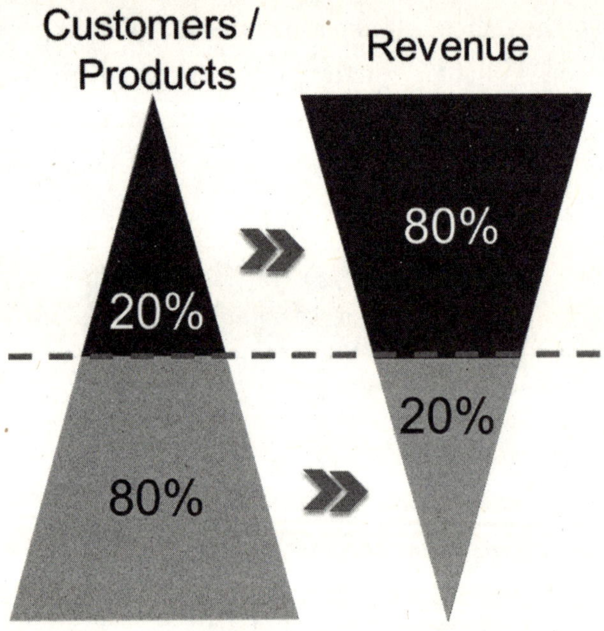

Figure 08-03

Pareto Principle illustrated by pyramids.

But there's another wrinkle, which requires the addition of another pyramid. The thing is, your best customers (the top 20%) account for just 20% of your overhead costs, which are ongoing business expenses that are not *directly* incurred in creating a product or service. If you are making aluminum foil, the cost of aluminum is a direct cost, but the business also must pay for insurance, rent or mortgage, utilities, accounting services, and other administrative expenses. These are overhead costs that apply to the entire business itself, rather than any particular product or customer. The thing is that the 80% of your customers who generate just 20% of your revenue account for 80% of your overhead costs. You cannot selectively allocate overhead. You are obliged to pay 100% of the overhead bill, 80% of which is de facto incurred by the customers who produce the trivial 20% fraction of your revenue. Figure 08-04 shows what this looks like.

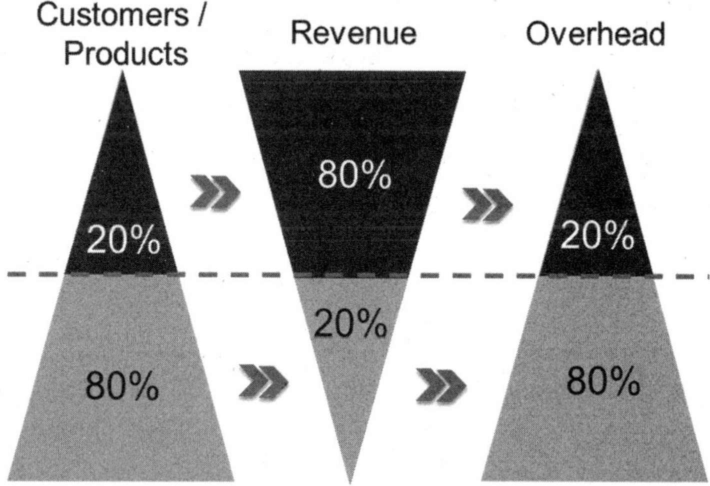

Figure 08-04

Pareto Principle with overhead costs added.

As the addition of the third pyramid makes clear, the revenue generated by your top 20% of customers (80%) comes at an overhead cost of just 20%, whereas the revenue generated by 80% of your customers (20%) costs 80% in overhead.

One hundred percent of overhead is a fixed and mandatory cost, a fact of business life. But you can ask, *What if the critical 20% of customers and the products they buy were my only customers and products?*

You can answer this thought experiment hypothetical by asking and answering this question: "What would it take in terms of cost to serve these critical few customers if they were my only customers?" To find out, you must restructure the business (hypothetically, of course) as a business selling only your critical few products to only your critical few customers. Here's a reality-based road to getting there:

Step 1: Segment your current business as it is to identify Quad 1: the Fort, the top 20% customer/product combinations that produce 80% of your revenue.

Step 2: Look at the head count actually employed in the business. The jobs of some are overhead functions, not directly related to acquiring, making, or selling your products. Set them aside, and consider only those directly involved in acquiring, making, or selling products or otherwise directly serving customers. Within this group, identify roughly the top 20% of performers, based on the sales numbers associated with them. Even without doing the thought experiment, you likely have a good idea of the top performers in your current organization.

Current—there's the rub. Your current (actual) organization serves much more than the top 20% of its customer/product combinations. You may know very well what it takes to serve 100% of your customers. The problem is that you don't (yet) know what is required to *optimally* serve—that is, overserve—the 20% who matter most.

Hold that thought. We must first finish outlining the steps toward discovering what it would take to serve these critical few customers if they were your only customers.

Step 3: Having already identified the customer/product combinations that belong in your Fort, move to that same quad all your top-performing employees directly involved in making, acquiring, or selling products. In your thought experiment, these folks now serve *only* your top-performing customer/product combinations.

Step 4: Fire (in your mind) everyone else—except for employees devoted to the mandatory overhead functions. Even among these employees you will be able to make cuts and reduce your overhead. Why? Because your company is now 80% smaller in size than it formerly was. For the purposes of the thought experiment, assume a perfect downsizing that will save you 80% on overhead.

Step 5: Run the numbers for your company, which is now downsized to serve only the top performers. Very likely, you will find that your scaled-down company is producing a 200% profit and maybe even more.

SCALE IT UP

Even a thought experiment needs to confront reality sooner or later. Otherwise, it becomes nothing more than science fiction. If you propose shrinking your company by 80%, you can be sure that you'll immediately meet with opposition. Up to this point, the experiment has been an exercise in what we can call creative destruction. We've cut away everything trivial, leaving only the critical core. Profit margin is higher, but revenue is lower because you have fewer customers.

Consider the idea of zeroing-up a monthly household budget. You list last month's expenses, identify every expense item you could do without, and retain only those absolutely necessary. This is your bare-bones budget for the next month. If you are on hard times, bare-bones may be mandatory rather than optional. You don't install a hot tub this week if you can't meet next month's mortgage. But maybe you have more financial headroom. In this case, you don't need to cut to the bone. You can budget for some *wants*, not just *needs*. Zeroing-up shows you where you must be financially to fund your *needs*. From this bare-bones base, you can add *wants* to the point that the costs exceed your income.

Applied to a business, a zero-up paints a counterfactual picture of how shedding 80% of your underperforming customer/product combinations produces a virtually frictionless business in which close to 100% of inputs prove to be nearly 100% critical instead of 20% critical and 80% trivial. Starting from this point, zeroing-up helps you to determine what it would take to *acquire* more A-customer/A-product combinations and also to move more B-customer/B-product combinations up from Quads 2 through 4, promoting these to A status.

The strategic objective of zeroing-up is to simplify the company by de-resourcing costly customer/product combinations with poor profitability while simultaneously overresourcing those with impactful profit share to gain. Done right, this 80/20 zero-up-based simplification will restructure the business by de-resourcing your P&L losers (shutting off the dollar spigot to them) and overresourcing your P&L winners (turning the service spigot to high).

Who are the losers? They are not bad folks or bad products. They simply have no meaningful profit share to gain. Resources allocated to these are therefore squandered. In contrast, the winners have a clear pathway to gaining share. Resources allocated to them will likely make the win even greater.

A 100% Quad 1 business does not exist in the real world. This does not mean you cannot act as if creating such a business were a realistic goal. Zeroing-up is invaluable in guiding the Visionary—in alignment with the Prophet(s) and the

Operators—to establish (or reestablish) the *necessary* level of resources to optimally serve the critical few (A customers buying A products) in preference to the trivial many. The mission is to eliminate or substantially reduce the destructively disproportionate volume of scarce resources required to serve underperforming and nonperforming products and customers, starting with those in the lowest customer/product quad, Quad 4.

REALLOCATE YOUR PRECIOUS RESOURCES—STRATEGICALLY

Establishing or reestablishing the level of resources *necessary* to serve the critical few in preference to the trivial many means reallocating assets, especially employees. Be bold in deploying or redeploying your top-performing employees from Quad 4 to Quad 1. More selectively, bring some of them to Quads 2 and 3.

Above all, *hold the Fort!* The high-performing customer/product combinations occupying Quad 1 must be over-resourced. Exceptional service does not merely retain the population of this quad, it grows it. Nevertheless, do not throw away Quads 2 and 3. To the extent that the customer/product combinations in these quads offer the prospect of meaningful profit share to gain (the possibility of lifting some customers and products from B to A status), serve these quads selectively by strategically deploying some of your best consultative sales employees to them. Compared to Quad 1, however, the business conducted in Quads 2 and 3 should be carried out as low-touch transactions, making extensive use of e-commerce and other modes of digital automation.

It is possible that the necessary reallocation can be accomplished with the human resources you have on hand. You even may need to hire additional personnel. Far more commonly, however, zeroing-up calls for "RIFs" (reductions in force), letting go of underperforming employees and shedding underperforming products. These two actions will doubtless result in some loss of customers. If the RIFs and inventory simplification are done with strategic skill, however, the customers you lose will be those you cannot afford to retain—underperforming customers who incur high costs for a service while producing little revenue.

BIG BITE OR SMALL BITES?

Zeroing-up is the next logical step after segmenting and simplifying. Many managers stop with the most basic application of 80/20 segmentation, but taking 80/20 to the next level via zero-up gives you more data-driven guidance to help turn the business around toward the right to grow. Zeroing-up gives you a more granular picture of how and where to deploy or redeploy resources. The 80/20 picture is standard definition—SD. The 80/20 picture + the zero-up vision is HD.

The businesses that benefit most from zeroing-up are those that are seemingly incapable of converting their B customers into A customers and their A customers into stark raving fans. With these businesses there are no quick fixes. In fact, turnaround is best achieved by starting from scratch.

A terrifying prospect. Well, take a deep, cleansing breath.

You don't need to take on the whole company. Proceed one segment at a time. I suggest not starting with your worst-performing segment, but with one that shows promise yet still has obvious and ample room for growth. Gather and work the data for that first segment. Run 80/20 on it, using only the resources available within the organization. Start with zero and build only what is needed to support this one segment's set of customers and products. Working patiently, a segment at a time, often reveals the hidden costs of complexity while simultaneously casting a light on places where costs can be reduced or removed entirely.

The great thing about taking on one segment at a time is that it thrusts the thought experiment into the real world. You learn how to effectively shift resources, de-resourcing the unproductive, and overresourcing the highly productive. By taking on one segment at a time, you will be able to make the trial-and-error aspect of PDCA work for you. As a one-segment trial solution proves itself, it can be scaled up, even through the entire company. You may want to focus on a market segment, a product segment, a region, or a business unit. What you are seeking is proof of concept: a prototype that can be applied to larger segments of the company or even to the entire company.

THE QUAD ZERO-UP

You need to find an approach that works well for you. For example, instead of lasering in on a single unit of the business, why not extend the Quad 1 thought experiment to the entire business? It can be done. You've already zeroed-up your Fort, Quad 1, by creating P&Ls for it as if it were the entire business. Go ahead and do the same in Quads 2 and 3.

What you want to do in each of these three separate quads (1, 2, and 3) is to build a P&L that demonstrates how to run each optimally—without regard to the others, as if each quad were the whole business. Now, as you create each of these scratch-built quads, track the spend required against the head count. When you have completed this thought experiment, you will have produced a separate optimal future-state P&L for each of the three quads, the head count needed to support each, and a running total. Then fit the three quads into the existing real-world company.

I haven't forgotten Quad 4. In this case, simplify it until you can wring some profit out of it.

PRODUCT/CUSTOMER INFLECTION POINT ZERO-UP

If you are prepared to roll up your sleeves, you can embark on a Product/Customer Inflection Point Zero-Up. This labor-intensive approach begins with composing a top-down list, starting with the best revenue-producing customer/product combination at the top and descending to the lowest at the bottom.

This list ranks customer/product pairs by revenue. The more meaningful measure of success, however, is profit. Determine who your most profitable customers are, and you can overresource them until you convert them into your raving fans. Don't stop. Convert even more A customers to raving status, and then convert more B customers to A status. To work at this level of granularity, you need to perform an Inflection Point Zero-Up analysis to find the line that separates profitable from unprofitable customers.

Run a thought experiment. You are the head of a newly minted company. Create a top-down customer list from your real company's data, snatch your best customer—number one on the list—and move that customer to the newborn company. Next, calculate the bare minimum cost required to support this one customer. You will want to factor in material costs, variable payroll, variable manufacturing overhead, fixed manufacturing overhead, SG&A (selling, general, and administrative) expenses, and other attached costs until you reach the EBITDA required to support this one best customer.

Go back to the list and make the same calculations for customer number two. Repeat this, customer by customer, all the way to the end of your roster.

When you are done, you will have compiled the EBITDA for each customer, along with a running total. You will find that, as successively lower-performing customers are added to the list, the increase in your running-total EBITDA for this new company begins to slow. If you plot the cumulative EBITDA, you will wind up with a very lumpy bell curve, which rises, fluctuates, and then flattens. At some point, the curve will inflect downward. The change will be obvious. It marks the inflection point at which *adding* lower-performing customers lowers the company's overall EBITDA. Generally, each customer added beyond this inflection further lowers overall EBITDA. There may be a few outliers. Some few customers at the lower end of the list will actually contribute positively to EBITDA. By the same token, on the high end of the revenue scale, some customers will depart from the general rule that the more productive a customer is, the more profitable.

When your list and curve are complete, reorder your customers by their EBITDA to yield a true bell curve without hills and valleys. Now, find the vertex of the curve, its highest point. The customers to the right of the vertex are eating away at your company's profitability. Everyone to the left is contributing to profit.

You will discover something even more remarkable. The 80/20 principle holds that 80% of your *revenue* comes from just 20% of your customer/product combinations, but this 20% is responsible for significantly more than 80% of your profits, typically 150% to 200%. That is how valuable they are to your business.

THE RIGHT TO GROW RATIO

Both quad zero-up and Product/Customer Inflection Point Zero-Up are opportune platforms for executing an 80/20 simplification, but you don't have to blindly obey the results of either analysis. Dropping customers and products is often advisable and even imperative, but you don't need to start with this scorched-earth approach. Heed your zero-up results but avoid acting on a reflex to chop, chop, chop. Remember the Dirty Dozen in chapter 7? It offers a wide choice of strategic alternatives to the chopping block.

Also consider applying one more calculation to your 80/20 segmentation and simplification. I call this the Right to Grow Ratio. Calculating it for business units, product lines, or other segments within your business or within an 80/20 quad—or even for the entire company—will give you the equivalent of a red/yellow/green traffic signal, which will aid decisions about how to strategically resource your business.

To find the Right to Grow Ratio for a given business segment, divide that segment's material margin by its total employee costs.

MATERIAL MARGIN AND TOTAL EMPLOYEE COSTS

To calculate Material Margin, divide gross profit by revenue, then multiply the result by 100 to obtain a percentage. Total employee costs include payroll plus taxes, benefits, travel, commissions, bonuses, insurance, and other direct employee outlays.

The Right to Grow Ratio is a straightforward measure of how a business segment converts inputs to outputs. It informs your zero-up actions with respect to earning the right to grow.

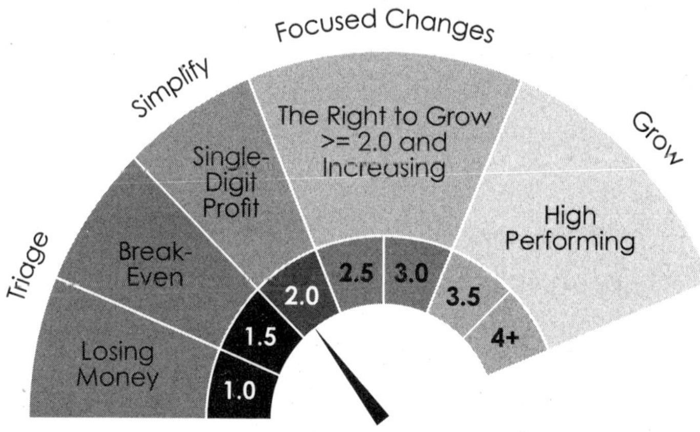

Figure 08-05

The Right to Grow Ratio.

On a four-point scale:

- Results of 3.5 to 4 (or greater) indicate a segment that should be overresourced to achieve growth. This is a green light for action.
- A result between 2.5 and 3.0 indicates that the segment should be sufficiently strategically resourced to move it toward growth. Often, this means resourcing sufficiently to promote a B customer/product combination to A status, thereby moving the combination from Quad 2 or 3 to Quad 1. Consider this a yellow light, advising you to take action to move toward growth, but with caution.
- 2.0 indicates a segment with a potential for low double-digit profit. Stop. Keep an eye on this segment. It may inflect downward or upward. If upward, consider resourcing for growth.
- 1.5 indicates a segment with a potential for no more than single-digit profit. Consider applying Dirty Dozen measures to move it toward greater profitability but be prepared to drop the segment altogether.
- 1.0 indicates a loser, a segment with little or no potential for profit.

Chapter 9

ALIGNMENT IS COMMITMENT, COMMITMENT IS ALIGNMENT

"Can two walk together, except they be agreed?"

—*Amos 3:3*

Everybody knows about D-Day, June 6, 1944, when American, British, and Canadian forces along with soldiers of other nations sailed across the English Channel and assaulted the beaches of Normandy, France. The landings, especially at the sector the Allies called Omaha Beach, were hard fought. The D-Day story is an epic of combat fought for the highest possible stakes. Little wonder that this event has been narrated in hundreds of history books and portrayed in scores of films.

Far less attention, however, has been devoted to the days and weeks following the landings and the establishment of beachheads. The next phase of the liberation of Europe was the long fighting advance through the interior of the continent. The troops had landed, along with their tanks and artillery. They faced a determined and skilled foe. But their most immediate adversary was what the French called the *bocage,* a countryside crisscrossed by high hedgerows, whose deep-sunk roots and thick woody branches overgrew the ancient stone walls that divided one farmer's field from the next. The combination of the vegetation and the stout stone walls created a seemingly unbreakable system of anti-tank obstacles. Allied armor advanced inland at an agonizing snail's pace. The vehicles and men, bogged down, were exposed to withering enemy fire. Worse, as the tanks labored up over each hedge-covered wall, their thinly armored bellies were exposed to enemy artillery while their own guns, pointing upward with the tank, could not be brought to bear.

Nobody—not General Omar Bradley, the top commander on the ground, and not General Dwight D. Eisenhower, the Supreme Allied Commander—could figure out what to do.

Enter Sergeant Curtiss Grubb Culin III, a tanker with the 102nd Cavalry Reconnaissance Squadron. He saw the problem firsthand. As he watched tanks ride over the hedgerows, exposing their vulnerable bottom decks, it occurred to him that what was needed was some way to push *through* rather than ride *over* the hedgerows. He discussed the matter with another soldier, known to history only by his last name, Roberts, who posed a simple question: "Why don't we get some saw teeth and put them on the front of the tank and cut through these hedges?"

Seemed impractical, but Culin couldn't get it out of his mind. He cobbled together a four-pronged plow out of steel scavenged from a German roadblock obstacle. He welded it to the front of his own Sherman tank and immediately began plowing huge gaps in the hedgerows. Having proved the concept, Culin put together a tusk-like assembly that could be welded to the front of each tank.

Figure 09-01

The "Culin Salad Fork" was an ingenious battlefield improvisation that enabled the American breakout through the Normandy hedgerow country after the D-Day landings.

In 1961, years after World War II, Eisenhower talked about Culin in one of his very last speeches as president of the United States:

> There was a little sergeant. His name was Culin, and he had an idea. And his idea was that we could fasten knives, great big steel knives, in front of these tanks, and as they came along they would cut off these banks right at ground level—they would go through on the level keel—would carry with themselves a little bit of camouflage for a while. And this idea was brought to the captain, to the major, to the colonel, and it got high enough that somebody did something about it—and that was General Bradley—and he did it very quickly. Because this seemed like a crazy idea, they did not even go to the engineers very fast, because they were afraid of the technical advice, and then someone did have a big question: "Where are you going to find the steel for all these things?" Well now, happily the Germans tried to keep us from going on the beaches with great steel "chevaux de frise" [steel obstacles]—big crosses . . . big bars of steel. [These were intended to rip out the bottoms of incoming landing craft. When the Germans retreated from the beaches, they left the obstacles behind.] And Culin collected them and . . . got these things sharpened up—and it worked fine. The biggest and happiest group I suppose in all the Allied Armies that night were those that knew that this thing worked. And it worked beautifully.

Ike was able to tell this story because news of Culin's invention traveled up the ranks, from captain, to major, and to a colonel, who took it to the top guy on the ground, General Bradley, who told General Eisenhower. Ike gave Bradley the order to equip as many Sherman tanks with what were now being called "Culin's salad forks."[3]

STAY IN YOUR LANE BUT LOOK LEFT AND RIGHT

The Rule of 3 is about defining essential roles, knowing your role, and playing that role—not someone else's. Visionaries have their lane, Prophets theirs, and Operators theirs. They travel in them, and the work gets done, with the necessary roles played and nobody stepping on anyone's toes. Military organization is a lot like this. General George S. Patton, for instance, believed in something very close to what advocates of Toyota's celebrated management practices call the Gemba Walk, or "management by walking around." He believed that officers—especially general officers, like himself—should get into the front lines and walk around, observe performance on the ground, firsthand. "I want every member of this staff to get up front at least once every day," he told his officers. "You will never know what is going on unless you

3 Max Hastings, *Overlord: D-Day and the Battle for Normandy* (Vintage, 2006), 296; and Omar Bradley, *A Soldier's Story* (Henry Holt, 1951), 342.

can hear the whistle of the bullets. You must lead the men. It is easier to lead than to push." But he was far from being a micromanager. He believed in training a person to do his or her job—and then getting out of the way. Patton wrote that senior commanders had a bad "habit of commanding too far down," and he explained this in detail:

> Actually, a General should command one echelon [level] down, and know the position of units two echelons down. For example, an Army Commander should command corps, and show on his battle map the locations of corps and divisions, but he should not command the division. A Corps Commander should command divisions and show on his map the location of combat teams. A Division Commander should command combat teams and show on his map the location of battalions . . . It has been my observation that any general officer who violates this rule and at, let us say, the Army level, shows the location of battalions, starts commanding them and loses his efficiency.

In essence: Walk around, see the action close up, what's working, what needs improvement, but don't do the work assigned to subordinate commanders.

The "Culin salad fork" certainly accelerated the breakout from the Normandy landing areas. It contributed to the Allied victory in World War II. In creating this innovation, Curtiss Culin acted as a Visionary. He looked out at scrap wreckage and envisioned not just a means of breaking through the deadly hedgerows—which was remarkable enough—but of doing so with the very obstacles the enemy had planted in the low water, where sea met shore, to tear out the hulls of Allied landing craft. It was an innovative and remarkably effective solution that cost nothing and only needed abandoned scrap as a raw material.

What a product! What a vision!

Yet President Eisenhower, speaking years later, characterized Culin as "a little sergeant," and the role of a sergeant is certainly not to be a Visionary. At best, a good sergeant is an Operator, seeing to it that those few troops under his command are fully aligned with and executing the mission. But while roles and ranks are strictly defined in the Army, Eisenhower's story demonstrates that the Army's structure and practices were sufficiently flexible to allow for a good idea to pass rapidly up the chain of command, from the captain of Culin's company, to the major in command of the battalion to which that company belonged, to the colonel in command of the regiment above the battalion, and to General Omar Bradley, at the time commanding the First US Army.

Bradley endorsed Culin's project with Eisenhower's approval. The lesson for leaders of business organizations is to implement the Rule of 3, ensuring that the organization has a Visionary, a Prophet or Prophets, and the complete complement of Operators suited to the nature, size, and structure of the business. At the same time, these leaders need to recognize that elements of each role can and should be manifested in anyone within the organization. Insights concerning strategy, processes, and implementation can come from anyone at any time. Be prepared to allow good ideas to permeate the membranes separating the three roles, and encourage insight to let them percolate upward. Rules are important, including the Rule of 3, and consistency is the integument and sinew of any successful organization. Nevertheless, in the words of Ralph Waldo Emerson, "A foolish consistency is the hobgoblin of little minds." Remain open, stay agile.

REMAIN OPEN. STAY AGILE

This admonition applies not just to the Rule of 3 but also to all other structured operational principles. Take DiSC, the enduringly popular personal assessment tool that is used to facilitate and improve teamwork and the productivity of workplace teams. The value of DiSC is *not* to "read people," label them, and then assign them roles in strict accordance with the label. Its true value is in creating a common language that people in the organization can use, first and foremost, to better understand themselves. The idea is that there is no better expert on you than you yourself. DiSC facilitates this understanding by providing a platform from which you can better understand those with whom you interact, to get work done more effectively while reducing conflict and improving working relationships.

We know from *DiSC* that—

- **People with *Dominant behavioral styles*** tend toward self-confidence and prize bottom-line results.
- **People with *influential behavioral styles*** tend toward openness, emphasizing influence to persuade others and build relationships.
- **People with *Supportive behavioral styles*** are typically dependable, prioritizing cooperation and sincerity.
- **People with *Conscientious behavioral styles*** stress quality, accuracy, expertise, and competency.

A person's DiSC profile essentially describes their typical or likely behavior in a given situation, as an aid to predicting performance. Obviously, it can help make decisions about assigning people to roles that suit them best. It also helps those assembling work teams to purposely recruit to provide a variety of behavioral types. On any team, the presence of people with complementary DiSC profiles is almost always a positive force—indeed, a force multiplier.

What we don't want to do is become dogmatic in the application of DiSC or other group-dynamics organizational and team-building profile tools. The utility of such tools is that they create greater clarity and mutual understanding in teams by getting everyone to speak a common language in describing personality, talents, strengths, weaknesses, preferences, and biases. Roles should never become straitjackets or prison sentences. Humphrey Bogart played great tough guys, but his own favorite movie role was as the neurotic Captain Queeg in *The Caine Mutiny.* The Irish actor Colin Farrell has played a lot of good-looking, charmingly roguish leading men, but, fattened up, scarred, and given a waddling limp, he turns in one of his most interesting performances as the oddly sympathetic mobster known in Batman's Gotham City as the Penguin. Team members may be assigned particular roles for very good reasons, but versatility is valuable and, sometimes, urgently needed.

As with all strategic decision making, thinking is required. Tools, processes, and rules are invaluable shortcuts to progress, but they are not inviolable commandments. They provide insight and a common language and are thus immensely useful in avoiding catastrophe, but when adhered to inflexibly, automatically, or without thought, rules can also lead you to miss opportunity. Prioritize resilience, agility, and an open mind.

THINK WIDE, THINK NARROW

While everyone in the enterprise must understand and align on the company's vision and values, *thinking is required.* Let's be precise here. As we saw in chapter 7, *two* kinds of thinking are required: divergent and convergent (see figure 07-05).

The two terms, *divergent thinking* and *convergent thinking,* were first proposed in 1956 by psychologist J. P. Guilford, who observed that some people, faced with a problem to solve, tend to brainstorm, generating multiple ideas and alternatives (divergent), while others tend to home in immediately on a single solution and then drill down to define it fully (convergent). Divergent thinking is typically associated with "creativity" and "imagination," whereas convergent thinking suggests the ascendency of logic over imagination. The venerable Myers-Briggs personality test, still very much in use among HR professionals, seeks to predict whether a candidate will be a "thinker" (making objective decisions based on data) versus a "feeler" (guided chiefly by subjective feelings and gut instincts). Thinkers are logical. Feelers are creative.

In practice, both divergent and convergent thinking are required—what's more, the same people must be willing and able to do both types of thinking. Now, some folks find divergent thinking exhilarating and playful. Others find it scary, overwhelming, and even a waste of time. In my experience, however, it is always best to generate a surplus of ideas by using divergent thinking at first. Once the team has gathered a range of opportunities, directions, and alternatives, it is time for expansive divergence to turn inward to the consolidation and streamlining of convergence. From *creating* endless choices, the focus turns to *making* specific choices. The discussions will likely become less energetic and more deliberate. Playfulness will morph into analysis, including sequencing, sorting, measuring, testing, and creating the *one* solution that seems best.

Divergent thought tends to be qualitative, whereas convergent thought is quantitative. Convergence taps the brakes and applies filters and a principle of selection. Objective analysis replaces subjective evaluation. Where divergence produces ideas, convergence selects some of them and reduces them to action. Discovery and definition, the province of divergent thought, transitions rapidly to development and delivery, the hallmarks of convergent thinking. What started as a search for abundance is now a project of unity, consensus, and alignment.

DIVERGE, CONVERGE, ALIGN, COMMIT

To some, the rhythm of divergent/convergent thinking seems wasteful. They ask: Why not focus fast, get a solution, and run with it? After all, isn't the objective of the Rule of 3 to achieve alignment? Why risk losing that alignment by insisting on diversity of thought—just to end up with convergence and consensus of thinking?

Maybe you remember from high school history class Roger Williams, the Puritan preacher who in the 17th century founded Providence Plantations—today's state of Rhode Island. While he was raised and educated as a Puritan, his advocacy of religious freedom—freedom of thought or, as he termed it, liberty of conscience or "soul liberty"—got him kicked out of the staunchly orthodox Massachusetts Bay Colony, prompting him to establish Providence Plantations as a haven for free thinking. As he colorfully proclaimed, "Forced worship stinks in God's nostrils."

While we seek alignment through Visionary, Prophet, and Operators, we must also take care not to force the alignment. I'm not going to tell you that forced alignment "stinks in God's nostrils," but let's just leave it at this: "Forced alignment stinks."

Why?

Because it's rotten and full of holes. And, in addition to failing the smell test, forced alignment is unsustainable, doomed to collapse sooner or later under its own weight. For this reason, thinking—divergent, followed by convergent—is required. As in any structure built to last, alignment of vision, strategy, and execution must be the resilient product of genuine, informed, voluntary, and enthusiastic consensus. Such consensus is best formed through the repeated diastole and systole of divergent and convergent thought, decisions made from a bounty of ideas and insights filtered down to the most productive: the 20% input of high value that will produce some 80% of the enterprise's revenue output.

This is the rhythm of profitable growth that is sustained by the Rule of 3 and that drives the four commandments of what I call the Winner's Calculus:

1. Be on pace: Meet all deadlines.
2. Let there be no surprises: Plan for all contingencies.
3. Be data driven: Act from facts.
4. Results matter: They are the proof of every concept and every strategy.

Epilogue: Always Be Exiting

Sabrina Horn, who founded, led, and after a quarter-century sold a boutique PR firm serving the B2B tech industry, wrote a book called *Make It, Don't Fake It.*[4] In it, she recommended that business owners should always run their business as if they were preparing to sell it. In other words, it is a great idea to think of your business as a product, merchandise, material thing or service to which you add sufficient value to persuade a customer to give you greater value in exchange for it.

Who doesn't remember the iconic cameo role Alec Baldwin contributed to the 1992 movie version of David Mamet's Broadway play *Glengarry Glen Ross*? Called in to motivate a group of burned-out, underperforming salesmen (and they are all men) hawking classically bad Florida real estate, Baldwin writes "ABC" on the chalkboard, standing for

---

4 Sabrina Horn, *Make It, Don't Fake It: Leading with Authenticity for Real Business Success* (Berrett-Koehler Publishers, 2021).

Always Be Closing. It's actually pretty good advice for sales professionals, although his notion of a motivational reward-for-performance contest leaves much to be desired. For the salesman who has the best quarter, first prize is a Cadillac, second prize is a set of crappy steak knives, and third prize is "*You're fired!*"

I am convinced that strategically managing a business calls for a slightly modified version of ABC, one that is in line with Sabrina Horn's advice. I call it ABE: *Always Be Exiting*. It is a call to start your business—or conceive a new vision for an existing business—by beginning with the end uppermost in mind.

If a business is a product—rather than a personal possession; a family legacy; or a monument to the founder's particular passion or set of moral, emotional, social, ethical, or political values—your mission is straightforward: Lead the business toward clear financial goals that add financial value to the enterprise, thereby making it attractive to a potential buyer. It matters less whether you eventually decide to sell the business than it does that you run the business, from the get-go, as if you intend to sell it. This controlling vision, the vision of the business as a product in a marketplace, aligns with a mission to profitably grow the company, relentlessly adding value to it so that a buyer will render even greater value to acquire it from you. Thus the mission summary, Always Be Exiting.

As I have pointed out, most of my business career has been spent as a CEO associated with private equity. The companies I lead are PE sponsored, so, generally speaking, my mandate is my mission, which is to add value to the business so that, within a certain time frame, it can be profitably sold. I like working this way. Ambiguity and ambivalence are energy-draining time sucks with too much room for questionable judgment, personal opinion, idiosyncrasy, outright bias, and "I don't know; what do you think?" Running a mission-focused company, especially when the mission is to add value through profitable growth, is hardly easy, but it is as near a thing to absolute as a business ever gets.

This doesn't mean that you must lead your business as a Mission company. As mentioned, the Mission company is only one of three general business models, along with the Values company and the Values & Mission company. Management must know which of these three business types they run. This awareness should be top of mind for the Visionary, Prophet(s), and Operators alike, all of whom must be in alignment on the company's priorities. This said, I believe that all three company types naturally benefit from the discipline of running the company as if you intend to sell it. Even a Values company, which does not prioritize profitable growth above all else, literally cannot afford to stand still, let alone consistently lose money—not, that is, if it wants to endure for the long term.

Compare this to the situation of owning a home. Most homeowners want to love their home. Toward this end, they maintain it and even improve it. Doing these things enhances the experience of simply living in that home. Of course, a home is not just a place to live but also an investment—usually the single biggest investment a family makes—and most homeowners want to add value to their house, both to make it more comfortable and pleasing to themselves, and more appealing to potential buyers.

Similarly, the owner/leader of a Values business may not want to enhance the financial worth of the company by sacrificing ethical or other values, but the fact is that these values are made more appealing and persuasive if they are linked to some degree of profitable growth. The idea that "nobody wants to buy my values-driven company" suggests that these values may simply not be widely perceived by others as attractive or desirable. Adding financial worth to such a company will likely raise the perceived attractiveness of the firm's ethical, moral, social, or intellectual values. In short, any business can benefit from leaders who run the organization as if they intend to sell it.

Likewise, any business will benefit from its Visionary's ABE mindset because it will drive a focus on continual *strategic* growth. The adjective *strategic* is key here. The ABE vision is not one of growth for growth's sake, but growth that is strategic in nature—that is, aligned with the priorities of the company. Those priorities are obvious in a Mission company: They all serve the addition of financial value. For the Values company, the addition of value—the growth—needs to be strategic, in service to its values. The same holds true for the Values & Mission company. Strategic growth aligns with the priorities and values of the company—that is where the strategy comes in—but strategic growth is growth.

Business, after all, is about change and transformation, not eternity. Tend to your business today as if you intend to sell it to someone else tomorrow. Develop this mindset, and you and your team will likely manage the enterprise in ways that put it in an optimal position.

The Visionary defines the vision of the company, but it requires the Rule of 3 to translate the vision into an executable mission, ensuring both are strategically aligned, and deploying them throughout the company. The Prophet translates the vision into the mission, much as the prophets of old translated the vision of the Creator into a religion, a mission and set of practices and processes by which the vision is realized and enacted. In a business, the Prophet inculcates and trains the Operators in the practices and processes by which the mission, aligned with the vision, is enacted on the ground.

The transformation of the vision through a mission that is executed strategically—that is, with optimal alignment rather than suboptimal idiosyncrasy—is not an automated cookie-cutter process that you set and forget. It requires continually monitoring, interrogating, and measuring income and outlays with the intention of creating progressive improvement. The ABE approach creates a mindset that provides the discipline to keep the processes and practices aligned with the mission across the organization. Here is an ABE checklist to help ensure that nothing is overlooked:

1. Continuously review and refine alignment on the vision throughout the company, but especially among the Visionary, Prophet(s), and Operators.
2. Continuously assess risks, opportunities, and top priorities. Evaluate and adjust alignment on these.
3. Continuously assess personnel and other organizational needs. Take action as needed to align on the vision, the strategy, and the execution.
4. Assign and continuously review responsibilities. Ensure accountability and ownership of each priority.
5. Communicate frequently to maintain alignment and to identify and resolve key concerns.
6. Be strategic in bonuses and other incentives, rigorously aligning these with priority targets.
7. Convene weekly leadership team meetings among management.
8. Convene monthly business reviews of sales and products.
9. Convene quarterly meetings with the executive leadership team.
10. Convene quarterly meetings ("town halls") with the entire organization.
11. Communicate regularly with the board concerning objectives and key areas of focus.
12. Keep telling your company's story—within the organization, to bankers and potential investors, to customers and consumers, to potential partners, and, yes, to potential buyers. Tell your story at every opportunity.

Neither the Prophet(s) nor the Operators create the vision or the mission, but they are essential to it. They enact the vision in the mission, for which they lead the practices and processes to successfully execute. They leverage the appropriate technologies that reduce the friction between strategy and execution, including the following:

- **Customer Relations Management systems**, to enhance the management of interactions with customers and ensure the collection and analysis of relevant data that allow the business to better understand its customers and address their needs and wants more effectively. Well-managed CRM is vital to retaining customers, creating new ones, and driving sales growth, all of which are critical to mission.
- **Enterprise Resource Planning systems**, to better enable the real-time alignment of many business activities within the organization. This technology can be crucial for both Prophets and Operators to help create and maintain optimal alignment among such activities as production, distribution, sales, customer service accounting, human resources, and corporate performance and governance. The evolution of cloud-based computing has vastly extended the power, reach, and real-time availability of key data across business activities and functions. Productive alignment begins and ends with information and its ready availability.

- **Material Requirements Planning (MRP)**, to enhance and accelerate the processes of production planning, scheduling, and inventory control to manage manufacturing processes, especially in lean environments, where just-in-time practices often make the difference between profit and loss. This technology has become essential to reducing uncertainty in supply chains and greatly limiting friction in fulfillment processes.
- **Manufacturing Resource Planning (MRP II)**, to extend MRP into a method and technology for strategically planning and managing all manufacturing resources in the business. While software systems greatly aid and accelerate these planning and coordination practices, they require dedicated managers. MRP and MRP II systems and personnel have become indispensable in manufacturing companies and are essential to lean operations. They are among the processes and practices that expedite the execution of vision, mission, and strategy while enabling highly effective feedback loops that allow real-time adjustments in performance.

Prophets and Operators ensure that the proper systems and practices are in place to carry out a mission aligned with the company vision. Add to this the value-multiplying mindset of ABE, and the organization will grow in value. If you are involved in a PE-sponsored company, the ABE mindset is virtually a condition of employment. These companies are not so much built to last as they are built to sell. If you run a Values or Values & Mission company, you may have no intention of selling, but it is nevertheless useful to behave and act as if you intend to sell it profitably. The ABE mindset not only produces improvement and increases engagement within the company; it makes your organization known to the outside world as something of great and growing value. It will make your story that much more compelling, both on Wall Street and Main Street.

Acknowledgments

Every idea in *The Rule of Three* was forged in real businesses, alongside real people who showed up every day to win. I've been fortunate to spend my career surrounded by incredible teams, partners, and mentors who taught me that leadership is never a solo act—it's a team sport.

To my teams at Arrowhead Engineered Products, OTC Industrial Technologies, and the many companies I've had the privilege to lead—thank you. You've taught me what it means to focus, to fight for simplicity, and to execute with discipline. The lessons in this book come straight from the front lines of our shared experience.

To my partners at Genstar Capital, I'm deeply grateful. Working with you has sharpened my thinking, challenged my assumptions, and reinforced that strategy without execution is just theory. You've helped me raise the bar on what great leadership looks like in practice.

To my friends and colleagues at The 80/20 Institute—thank you for turning frameworks into action and helping leaders around the world find clarity and focus. Your passion for the mission keeps me moving forward.

To my family—Debbie, Sarah, Hannah, Collin, and Nico—you are my anchor. Your love, patience, and belief make everything possible. You've given me the strength to keep going, even when the work seemed endless.

And finally, to every leader who picks up this book—thank you for caring enough to get better. Leadership is hard work, and it's worth every ounce of effort. My hope is that *The Rule of Three* gives you the tools and confidence to lead with clarity, build teams that win, and earn the right to grow—again and again.

Photography Credits

Images on pages 4, 7, and 11 from USAAF.

Image on page 36 © CC-BY-2.0 Generic. PEO ACWA.

Images on page 38, 62, 90, 119, 183 in public domain.

Image on page 41 © CC-BY-2.0 Generic. Joi Ito.

Image on page 45 © CC-BY-4.0 International. ZDF/Terra X/Gruppe 5/ Susanne Utzt, Cristina Trebbi/ Jens Boeck, Dieter Stürmer / Fabian Wienke / Sebastian Martinez/ xkopp, polloq.

Image on page 60 © CC-BY-Share Alike 3.0 Unported. Ygrek.

Image on page 87 © CC-BY-Share Alike 2.0. Jeff McNeill.

Image on page 107 © CC-BY-4.0 International. Wiki Science Competition 2017.

Image on page 126 by Hay Kranen / PD.

Image on page 172 © CC-BY-4.0 International. Diagram by Karn Bulsuk.

Image on page 201 from U.S. Army Signal Corps Archive.

About the Author

The author of *From Panic to Profit: Uncover Value, Boost Revenue, and Grow Your Business with the 80/20 Principle* (Wiley, 2025) and *The 80/20 CEO: Take Command of Your Business in 100 Days* (Köehlerbooks, 2024), Bill Canady has worked for over thirty years as a global business executive across a variety of industries and markets focused on industrial and consumer products and services. He is CEO of two companies, with a combined revenue of $2.5 billion. As CEO of OTC Industrial Technologies, a private equity–sponsored company, he directs an organization with 30 operating companies, $1 billion in annual sales, 2,000+ employees, and over 70 sites.

Bill has led numerous organizations through their most critical challenges and opportunities, often in complicated regulatory, investor, and media environments. Through his long career, he has honed a passion for the art and science of business, developing a set of tools and techniques to grow multibillion-dollar companies. From this experience, he created the Profitable Growth Operating System® (PGOS) and has set out to help owners and operators around the world profitably grow their companies.